WRITE SOURCE
2000
SkillsBook
Editing and Proofreading Practice

. . . a resource of student activities
to accompany the
Write Source 2000 and
All Write handbooks

D1472597

WRITE SOURCE®

GREAT SOURCE EDUCATION GROUP
a Houghton Mifflin Company
Wilmington, Massachusetts

A Few Words About the
Write Source 2000 SkillsBook

Before you begin . . .

The *SkillsBook* provides you with opportunities to practice the editing and proofreading skills presented in the *Write Source 2000* and *All Write* handbooks. The handbooks contain guidelines, examples, and models to help you complete your work in the *SkillsBook*.

Each *SkillsBook* activity includes a brief introduction to the topic and examples illustrating how to complete that activity. You will be directed to the page numbers in the handbook for additional information and examples. The "Proofreading Activities" focus on punctuation and the mechanics of writing. The "Sentence Activities" provide practice in sentence combining and in correcting common sentence problems. The "Language Activities" highlight each of the eight parts of speech.

The Next Step

Most activities include a **Next Step** at the end of the exercise. The purpose of the Next Step is to provide ideas for follow-up work that will help you apply what you have learned to your own writing.

Important Note: If you are using this *SkillsBook* with the *All Write* handbook, refer to the handbook numbers at the bottom of each page. The numbers are printed in color.

Authors: Pat Sebranek and Dave Kemper

Trademarks and trade names are shown in this book strictly for illustrative purposes and are the property of their respective owners. The authors' references herein should not be regarded as affecting their validity.

Printed in the United States of America

International Standard Book Number: 0-669-46776-6 (student edition)

2 3 4 5 6 7 8 9 10 - POO - 04 03 02 01 00 99

International Standard Book Number: 0-669-46779-0 (teacher's edition)

2 3 4 5 6 7 8 9 10 - POO - 04 03 02 01 00 99

Table of Contents

Proofreading Activities

Sentence Activities

Sentence Basics

Sentence Combining

Sentence Problems

Sentence Variety

Language Activities

Proofreading
Activities

Every activity in this section includes sentences that need to be checked for punctuation, mechanics, or correct word choices. Most of the activities also include helpful handbook references. In addition, the **Next Step** activities encourage follow-up practice of certain skills.

End Punctuation 1

Periods, exclamation points, and question marks are used at the ends of sentences. Usually, these marks will mean that you have come to the end of a complete thought—either a statement or a question. (Turn to 387.1, 398.1, and 398.4 in *Write Source 2000* for more information.)

EXAMPLES

People must sleep to stay healthy.
(A period marks the end of a complete thought.)

How many hours of sleep do we need each day?
(A question mark indicates a question.)

My older brother once slept for 12 straight hours!
(An exclamation point expresses strong feelings or emphasis.)

Directions **Put periods, question marks, and exclamation points where they are needed in the following paragraphs. Also supply the needed capital letters at the beginnings of sentences. The first two sentences have been done for you.**

1 You know, of course, that people need to sleep. Have you ever

2 heard that if you work hard during the day, you'll sleep well during

3 the night?

4 That belief is wrong scientists now feel that the need for sleep

5 has little to do with your physical state it's your brain that needs

6 sleep, and it will not function normally for long without sleep it is

7 now known that people need to dream in order to maintain healthy

8 brains

9 Scientists have found that everyone dreams if people do not

10 dream, their brains will begin to malfunction if you go without

All Write pp. 311-312

11 dreaming, you will become very irritable after a while, you may even

12 suffer memory loss the effects of dreamlessness may last for weeks or

13 months just think about that

14   Why is dreaming so necessary scientists are not sure of the

15 answer during sleep, the brain really doesn't rest it is very active all

16 night long the brain needs the special kind of activity it gets while

17 you sleep

18   You need to help your brain function properly don't stay up late

19 to watch TV or do homework do some good dreaming instead

Next Step Write a paragraph about a time when you were really tired, but you had to stay awake. Use all three kinds of end punctuation in your paragraph—periods, question marks, and exclamation points.

End Punctuation 2

Periods, question marks, and exclamation points are used to mark the ends of sentences; but periods have other uses also. (Turn to page 387 in *Write Source 2000* for all the rules covering periods. Also read "Placement of Punctuation," 400.1.)

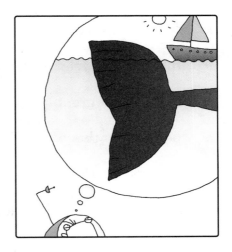

Directions

Place periods, question marks, and exclamation points where they belong in the following narrative. Add capital letters to the beginnings of sentences. The first two corrections have been done for you.

1   *D*id you know that the world's largest animal lives in the water?

2   it's the blue whale this type of whale sometimes weighs nearly 200

3   tons that's twice as heavy as the biggest dinosaur that ever lived Peter

4   J Fromm tells some amazing stories about this gentle giant in his

5   book *Whale Tales: Human Interaction with Whales*

6   The blue whale can survive for six months without eating a thing

7   how does it do that it lives off its own blubber wouldn't you think

8   that this huge creature would go after a shark or an octopus when it

9   is hungry no, the blue whale is a vegetarian it exists completely on a

10   diet of microscopic plants called zooplankton

11   Endangered whales include blue whales, humpback whales, fin

12   whales, and sperm whales in the 1970's an organization called

13   Greenpeace drew attention to the plight of whales everywhere this

14   organization tried to get whaling stopped how did they do this

All Write pp. 311 and 324

15   Greenpeace created media stunts they placed a small inflatable

16   lifeboat between a large whaling vessel and the whale it was hunting

17   this made great pictures for television and newspapers and got many

18   people on the whales' side

19   "Save the whales" became a common battle cry people who hadn't

20   thought much about whales before joined the crusade bumper stickers

21   carried the message across the country

22   All of this publicity led to a ban on commercial whaling for five

23   years not every country agreed to the ban, but whaling was

24   dramatically decreased the gigantic blue whale now has a chance to be

25   around for many centuries hurrah for the whales

Next Step Look for animal facts in the "Student Almanac" in your handbook. What other animals have the same names as the whale for the male, female, and young of their species? Without researching the topic, write a paragraph that explains why *you* think these three species share names.

Punctuating Dialogue 1

A conversation in writing is called *dialogue*. There are special rules for using quotation marks, commas, and end punctuation marks when you are punctuating dialogue. (Turn to 399.1, 399.2, and 400.1 in *Write Source 2000* for more information.)

EXAMPLES

"I'm bored," said Clara. "Let's go shopping."
(A period comes after *Clara* because that's the end of a complete sentence.)

"Oh yeah," joked Keith, "I'd just love to get a new dress."
(A comma comes after *Keith* because what follows completes the sentence.)

"What you really need, Keith, is a new address!" Clara shot back.
(The exclamation point is inside the quotation marks because the quotation is an exclamation.)

Directions Punctuate the following examples of dialogue with quotation marks, commas, and end marks. The first sentence has been done for you.

1   "Hey, Joe, there's a bee on your back! yelled Carlyle. Hold still

2   while I swish it away

3   Everyone be quiet and take your seats said Mr. Beech

4   But what about the bee said Joe I could be seriously stung

5   Just sit still. It won't sting you if you stop jumping around

6   advised Mr. Beech

7   Besides added Carlyle it's a known fact that bees only sting living

8   objects

9   Real funny, Carlyle. Now just get it off me pleaded Joe.

All Write pp. 311-312, 323-324

Punctuating Dialogue 2

When you are writing dialogue, you have to start a new paragraph each time the speaker in a conversation changes. (Turn to 399.1 and 400.1 in *Write Source 2000* for more information.)

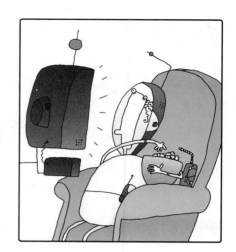

Directions   Add quotation marks, commas, and end punctuation as needed. The first sentence has been done for you.

1   "What's there to do around here? José asked.

2   Why don't you do something to improve your mind suggested his

3   father. Here's an article about native wildflowers that you could read

4   Uh, thanks, Dad José said That sounds fascinating

5   What about reading short stories such as A Start in Life from

6   your literature text asked his mom. I'm sure you won't read them all

7   in class

8   I've been dying to do that José said but I'm already trying to finish

9   three chapters in my social studies book

10   You could attend a lecture at the community center his older

11   brother volunteered. I heard that the basket weaving session is

12   awesome.

13   You guys are really helpful said José but I have to go. I just

14   remembered I have to watch a video I rented. See you later.

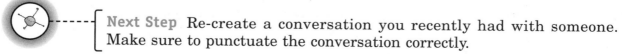

Next Step Re-create a conversation you recently had with someone. Make sure to punctuate the conversation correctly.

All Write pp. 311-312, 323-324

Commas in a Series

Commas are used to separate a series of three or more words, phrases, or clauses. They are also used in big numbers. (Turn to 389.1 and 389.2 in *Write Source 2000* for more information and examples.)

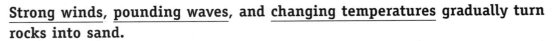

EXAMPLES

Sand is made up of tiny pieces of <u>rocks</u>, <u>shells</u>, and <u>lava</u>.
(Commas are used to separate words in a series.)

<u>Strong winds</u>, <u>pounding waves</u>, and <u>changing temperatures</u> gradually turn rocks into sand.
(Commas are used to separate phrases in a series.)

<u>Waves pound against the coastline</u>, <u>water freezes in the cracks of the rocks</u>, and <u>the rocks split apart</u>.
(Commas are used to separate clauses in a series.)

Collecting <u>1,000,000</u> sand dollars won't make you rich.
(Commas are used to keep big numbers clear.)

Directions   Use commas correctly in the sentences below. The first sentence has been done for you.

1. The five largest deserts in the world are the Sahara, the Australian, the Arabian, the Gobi, and the Patagonian.

2. These deserts are found in North Africa Australia Southwest Asia Central Asia and South America.

3. The Sahara Desert covers 9 0 6 5 0 0 0 square kilometers the Gobi Desert covers 1 2 9 5 0 0 0 square kilometers and Death Valley in the United States covers only 7 8 0 0 square kilometers.

4. Deserts are made up of rocks gravel or sand.

   All Write p. 313

5. Death Valley is the driest hottest and lowest place in North America.

6. Over the course of time, the Sahara has been covered by ice seawater forests and grass.

7. Sandstorms have been known to whip up the sand as high as 1 0 0 0 0 feet with the power to sandblast the paint off a car a truck or an airplane.

8. The Gobi Desert is located on the border between China and Mongolia and lies on a plateau that is between 2 9 5 0 and 4 9 2 0 feet high.

9. Fossilized eggs bones and the skeleton of a giant tyrannosaur have been found in the Gobi Desert.

10. The world's deserts are growing because of improper farming mining and the destruction of trees.

Next Step What are the hottest places that you have ever lived in or visited? Write a sentence that includes a list of these places (punctuated with commas, of course). Then write a paragraph that describes one of these places using lists of words, phrases, and clauses.

Commas Between Independent Clauses

A comma is used between two independent clauses that are joined by a coordinating conjunction. (Turn to 391.1 in *Write Source 2000* for more information.)

EXAMPLE

People have always dreamed of flying, *but* the earliest recorded flight took place in 1793.

(A comma is used between two independent clauses joined by the coordinating conjunction *but*.)

Directions   Add commas to the sentences below. The first sentence has been done for you.

1. The Montgolfier brothers were the first to fly in a hot-air balloon, and people were astonished.

2. No one thought the Wright brothers' flying machine would work, but that didn't stop the brothers from trying.

3. Their airplane was called *Flyer I* and it flew for a full 12 seconds.

4. *Flyer I* flew less than 100 feet yet it put the Wright brothers in the history books.

5. Today, the Concorde aircraft flies at twice the speed of sound and it can cross the Atlantic in less than three hours.

6. Each year, nearly a billion people fly on airplanes and that's just on commercial flights.

7. It will soon be possible to "fly" anywhere in the world and you'll be able to do it all on the Internet.

   All Write p. 316

Directions	Complete the following sentences with a comma, a conjunction, and a second independent clause. The first one has been done for you.

1. Neither the Montgolfier brothers nor the Wright brothers would believe it

   but air travel is now a normal part of everyday life.

   _____

2. My brother has flown three times

   _____

   _____

3. Flying is a very safe form of transportation

   _____

   _____

4. The Concorde is the fastest passenger plane today

   _____

   _____

5. Some big planes hold more than 300 people

   _____

   _____

6. Stunt flying seems very scary

   _____

   _____

Next Step Write a paragraph about some other form of transportation. Use at least three compound sentences (independent clauses joined by commas and coordinating conjunctions).

Commas After Long Phrases and Clauses

Commas are used to separate long phrases and clauses from the rest of a sentence. Commas are also used to separate two or more adjectives that equally modify the same noun. (Turn to 391.2 and 391.3 in *Write Source 2000* for more information.)

EXAMPLES

<u>After a long period of time</u>, the origin of a piece of music is often forgotten.
(A comma is placed after a long introductory phrase.)

<u>When people write classical music</u>, they are called composers.
(A comma is placed after an introductory clause.)

Not all composers are <u>trained, professional</u> musicians.
(Place commas between two or more adjectives that equally describe the same noun.)

Directions   Add commas to the following sentences. If the sentence is already correct, write *correct* on the line. The first sentence has been done for you.

1. _____ Although you may find it hard to believe‸"Chopsticks"
was actually composed by someone.

2. _____ Loud pounding versions of "Chopsticks" have been played by many beginning pianists.

3. _____ The person who created "Chopsticks" was a talented high-strung teenager from Great Britain named Euphemia Allen.

4. _____ When the tune first appeared in 1877 it was called "The Celebrated Chopsticks Waltz, Arranged as a Duet and Solo for the Pianoforte."

All Write pp. 316-317

5. _____ Then the long complicated name of the piece was shortened to simply "Chopsticks."

6. _____ As a matter of clarification, "pianoforte" is just a fancy name for "piano."

7. _____ You might think that "Chopsticks" was named after the long thin eating utensils used by the Chinese.

8. _____ As a matter of fact the name "Chopsticks" comes from the chopping motion the fingers make while playing this music.

9. _____ At the time that Euphemia wrote her "masterpiece" one-finger piano pieces were popular with children.

10. _____ Little did she know that she was composing such a timeless universal piece of music.

Next Step Write a paragraph that explains how to play a musical instrument, a sport, or a game. Use at least two long introductory phrases or clauses, such as "Before you pick up the bat, . . . " or "After placing both hands on the keyboard, . . . ".

Commas with Explanatory Phrases

Commas are used to set off phrases that explain or rename nouns. (Turn to 391.4 and 392.1 in *Write Source 2000* for more information.)

EXAMPLES

Islam, <u>a religion founded in Arabia in the seventh century</u>, has well over 1 billion followers.
(Commas are used to separate an explanatory phrase from the rest of the sentence.)

Muhammad, <u>the founder of Islam</u>, died in A.D. 632.
(Commas also separate an appositive from the rest of the sentence. An appositive renames the noun it follows.)

Directions   Add commas to the sentences below. If a sentence is already correct, write *correct* on the line. The first sentence has been done for you.

1. _____ Muslims͵followers of Islam͵created a huge empire.

2. _____ The Islamic Empire once stretching from Spain to China brought with it the Arabic language, culture, and the Islamic religion.

3. _____ Mecca, the birthplace of Muhammad, is located in western Saudi Arabia.

4. _____ All Muslims try to make the hajj a pilgrimage to Mecca at least once in their lifetimes.

5. _____ The Koran the Muslims' holy book contains the teachings of Muhammad.

6. _____ People are called to pray five times a day in mosques Muslim holy buildings.

All Write pp. 317-318

7. _____ Arabic, the language of the Koran, is one of the major languages of the world.

8. _____ Islam a religion common throughout Africa has over 5 million followers in the United States.

9. _____ Kareem Abdul Jabbar a former professional basketball player is a follower of Islam.

10. _____ The symbol of Islam a crescent and star appears on many national flags.

Next Step Write five sentences that contain appositives for people that you know. For example, *Mr. Jackson, my favorite teacher, is a mathematical genius.* (Don't forget to use commas correctly.)

Commas with Nonrestrictive Phrases and Clauses

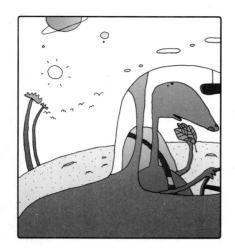

A phrase or clause that is not needed to complete the meaning of a sentence is called a **nonrestrictive phrase** or **clause**. A nonrestrictive phrase or clause adds "extra" information and is set off with commas. A phrase or clause that is needed to complete the meaning of a sentence is called a **restrictive phrase** or **clause.** A restrictive phrase or clause is not set off with commas. (Turn to 392.2 in *Write Source 2000*.)

EXAMPLES

Nonrestrictive Phrase:

Many things, <u>from leaves to dinosaurs</u>, can become fossils.

(The underlined phrase is *nonrestrictive*; the meaning of the sentence is complete without it.)

Restrictive Clause:

Anything <u>that can be preserved for a long time</u> can become a fossil.

(The underlined clause is *restrictive*; the meaning of the sentence is not complete without it.)

Directions   This activity gives you practice identifying nonrestrictive and restrictive phrases and clauses. On the line before each sentence below, write whether the underlined phrase or clause is *nonrestrictive* or *restrictive.* The first sentence has been done for you.

nonrestrictive **1.** Sharks, <u>which do not have bones</u>, do not leave fossils.

_____ **2.** The soft cartilage <u>that makes up sharks' skeletons</u>

dissolves over time.

_____ **3.** The only part of a shark <u>that lasts for thousands of years</u>

is its teeth!

All Write p. 318

_____ **4.** Recently scientists found the first fossils of Gigantosaurus, which means "monstrous lizard."

_____ **5.** Gigantosaurus, which lived in South America, was even bigger than Tyrannosaurus rex.

_____ **6.** Rancho La Brea Tar Pit and Dinosaur National Monument are two places that have a lot of dinosaur fossils.

_____ **7.** Many insects become fossilized when they get stuck in amber.

_____ **8.** David Shiffler, who was born in 1992, is already a famous fossil finder.

_____ **9.** On a camping trip when he was three, David found something that he thought was a dinosaur egg.

_____ **10.** David's father didn't believe him, but David was right, according to a fossil expert.

_____ **11.** Emily Bray, a fossil expert, said the egg that David found was 150 million years old.

Next Step Each sentence below has one nonrestrictive phrase or clause and one restrictive phrase or clause. Write _N_ above each nonrestrictive phrase or clause and _R_ above each restrictive phrase or clause.

1. Petoskey stones, which are found in Petoskey, Michigan, have fossils that can only be seen when the stones are wet.

2. Explorers Lewis and Clark, when they were in Montana, found dinosaur bones that they thought were the bones of huge elephants.

Comma Practice 1

Commas are used to separate words, phrases, or clauses in sentences. Commas make writing easier to read. (Turn to pages 389-392 in *Write Source 2000*.)

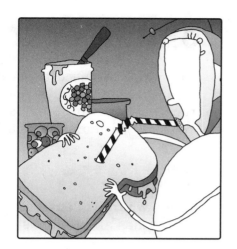

EXAMPLES

After I drank the entire quart of orange juice, I sat down and "died."
(The comma after *juice* separates an adverb clause from the main sentence, or independent clause, that follows it.)

I like grape jam, cream cheese, and green olives on a sandwich.
(The commas separate a series of words.)

My brother likes peanut-butter sandwiches, but I think they're boring.
(The comma separates two independent clauses.)

Directions   Read the paragraph that follows and add commas where you think they are needed. Use the examples above as your guide.

1   I use a computer for producing final drafts but I can't actually

2   write on it. I turn it on listen to it boot up put my fingers on the

3   keyboard, and then . . . nothing. On the other hand writing on paper

4   makes me feel as if I can conquer the whole world. When I see the

5   ink on the page I know I'm making my mark. The words are like

6   clay in my hands and I can rework them until they're right. I may

7   change words two three or four times before I am satisfied. On the

8   computer screen words seem to be written in stone. They stare at me

9   with impersonal eyes and I find it difficult to work with them.

Next Step Exchange your work with a classmate and check each other's work. If you have questions, refer to your handbook.

All Write pp. 313-318

Comma Practice 2

Commas are used to set off interjections, nouns of direct address, and words and phrases that interrupt a sentence. (Turn to 390.2, 390.3, and 390.4 in *Write Source 2000* for more information.)

EXAMPLES

Hey, where is Pensacola?
(Commas are used to set off interjections.)

Jim, Pensacola is in Florida.
(Commas are used to set off nouns of direct address.)

More specifically, Pensacola is in western Florida.
(Commas are used to set off a word, phrase, or clause that interrupts a sentence.)

Directions Add commas to the sentences below. The first sentence has been done for you.

1   "Jim, have you ever heard of a city named Peculiar in Missouri?"

2   "No I've heard of Normal, Illinois, but not Peculiar, Missouri."

3   "As a matter of fact Jim lots of U.S. towns have unusual names."

4   "Yes I know. For example there's a town called Why in Arizona."

5   "Hmm that's pretty close to Whynot, Mississippi."

6   "Right Joe. Do you think it's safe to live in Accident, Maryland?"

7   "Hey I wouldn't risk it. By the way I wonder if all the folks in

8   Library, Pennsylvania, and in Magazine, Arkansas, are good readers."

Next Step Continue this conversation between Joe and Jim. Add two more sentences with funny or interesting place-names. Use direct address *(Joe, Jim)*, interrupters *(for example)*, and interjections *(hey, no kidding)*.

Comma Practice 3

Here's a chance for you to practice four important uses of commas. Review the examples below before you begin your work. (Also turn to 389.1, 390.2, and 391.1-392.2 in *Write Source 2000* for more examples.)

EXAMPLES

(A) A comma is used between two independent clauses connected with a coordinate conjunction (a compound sentence):
I work very hard from Monday through Friday, but I enjoy myself on weekends.

(B) Commas separate items in a series:
Attending school, going to soccer practice, and completing homework take up all of my time during the week.

(C) A comma separates a long introductory phrase or clause from the rest of the sentence:
When Friday night arrives, I'm totally exhausted.

(D) Commas set off phrases that interrupt the main thought:
In fact, I'm so tired that I usually fall asleep really early.

Directions | Find the rule (*A, B, C,* or *D*) that applies to the commas used in the first six sentences below. Write the correct letter on the lines. For the last five sentences, you must supply the commas and the letters. The first sentence has been done for you.

1. __*B*__ I like shopping, reading, and playing badminton on weekends.

2. _____ My mother, on the other hand, loves to take piles of work home with her.

3. _____ I would love to go to the movies, but I have my final soccer match.

4. _____ When I wake up on Saturday morning, I head straight for the sweet rolls in the kitchen.

5. _____ I have to pick up my room, clear the kitchen table, and walk the dog before I can go out.

All Write pp. 313-318

6. _____   Although Josie is my best friend at school, I do more things with Anna on weekends.

7. _____   When I see blue sky through my window I always feel like smiling.

8. _____   Lawrence could finally catch his breath after taking a shower rushing through breakfast and running to his game.

9. _____   Jackie watched three movies believe it or not before she developed a major headache.

10. _____   My mother often tells me I'm pretty yet I try to hide behind my hair.

11. _____   In the last part of fall I like to rake up huge piles of leaves and jump in them.

| Directions | Write original sentences according to the directions provided below. (Make sure to use commas correctly in your sentences.) |

1. Write a compound sentence using the connecting word *but.*

_____

_____

2. Write a sentence that includes a series of words or phrases.

_____

_____

3. Write a sentence that includes a long introductory phrase or clause.

_____

_____

4. Write a sentence that includes a phrase that interrupts the sentence's main thought.

_____

_____

Semicolons and Colons

Both semicolons and colons have several uses, including the ones shown in the examples below. Study these examples and the ones in *Write Source 2000* (393.1-394.5) before you start your work.

EXAMPLES

Quartz is the most common mineral found in the world; ordinary sand is made up mostly of quartz.
(A semicolon can be used to join two independent clauses that are not connected with a coordinate conjunction—*and, or, but.*)

There are many varieties of quartz: agate, amethyst, flint, jasper, onyx.
(A colon can be used to introduce a list.)

Quartz is a very hard mineral; however, it is not as hard as diamond.
(A semicolon is used to join two independent clauses when the clauses are connected by a conjunctive adverb—*however, therefore, as a result, for example,* etc.)

A geologist named David Vister stated this fact: "Erosion does not wear away quartz as rapidly as most other rock materials."
(A colon may be used to formally introduce a quotation.)

Directions   Add semicolons and colons to the sentences below. The first sentence has been done for you.

1. The earth contains many kinds of minerals; moreover, some of the same minerals have been found on the moon, on other planets, and in meteorites.

2. Quartz is used in making the following items watches and clocks, heat-resistant glass, microscope lenses, and sandpaper.

3. Minerals are solid, nonliving materials in the soil rocks are combinations of minerals.

        All Write pp. 319-320

4. There are three kinds of rocks igneous, sedimentary, and metamorphic.

5. Granite, marble, and quartzite are considered hard rocks limestone, sand, and shale are considered soft rocks.

6. Geologists study rocks by drilling deep into the crust of the earth they also use aerial photography and satellites to get information about the earth's surface.

7. Not every precious gem comes from minerals for example, pearls come from oysters, which are living things.

8. The most precious stones are the following emeralds, rubies, sapphires, and diamonds.

9. Both diamonds and graphite pencils are made of carbon however, diamonds are certainly much more valuable.

10. Mrs. MacIntosh made this claim "I love carbon. I never go anywhere without my diamond ring or my pencil."

Next Step Have you ever noticed how many things are made of cement— pulverized minerals mixed with sand? Write a paragraph in which you imagine a world without cement. What would be missing? How would your life be different? Use at least one colon to introduce a list, and a semicolon to join two independent clauses.

Dashes and Hyphens

Dashes are used to show a sudden break or interruption in a sentence and to emphasize a word, a phrase, or a clause. **Hyphens** are used to divide a word between its syllables and to join words for different reasons. Study the examples below plus the examples in the handbook before you work on this activity. (Turn to 395.1-395.3 and 396.1-397.3 in *Write Source 2000*.)

EXAMPLES

I bought a pack of gum—I think it was gum—at the store.
(Dashes are used to show an interruption in a sentence.)

My pet peeve is waiting—waiting for supper, waiting for tickets, waiting at checkout counters.
(A dash can be used to emphasize the words that follow.)

My all-time record for a grocery purchase was three and one-half seconds.
(Hyphens are used to join two or more words used as a single adjective. They are also used in spelled-out fractions.)

Directions Add hyphens and dashes to the paragraphs that follow. The first sentence has been done for you.

1   Now, I'm not one to complain about high-tech gadgets. I'm a red

2   blooded, all American girl. I love computers and anything that will

3   save me three fourths of a second. While my mother bless her heart

4   stands in an actual line to check out books at the library, I zip my

5   library card through the self scanner. She says she doesn't trust the

6   scanner, but I think she's just old fashioned and worried that she

7   won't do it right.

8   By the time you read this article, self scanning devices, which

9   were introduced in 1998, will be in many stores. Storekeepers say that

All Write pp. 321-322

10 scanning provides hassle free shopping.

11   When customers finally make their decisions, they don't want to

12 wait in mile long lines just to pay for their purchases. You scan your

13 own purchases, drop them into a bag, get a receipt, and then get in

14 line to pay a cashier. (This line thankfully, a very short one moves

15 quickly.)

16   The scanner even prevents not so honest customers from dropping

17 little "extras" into their bags. It checks to see that everything you drop

18 into your store provided bag matches the weight down to the last

19 milligram of the item you just scanned. Satisfied customers and that's

20 what we all want to be say scanning offers the quickest shopping

21 experience ever. There is just one thing that I wonder about. What

22 will we do with all the minutes maybe even hours that we save?

Next Step Write a paragraph about a recent shopping experience. Use at least one set of dashes and one hyphen in your work. Afterward, share your writing with a classmate. Check each other's use of these two marks of punctuation.

Apostrophes 1

Apostrophes are used to form contractions, to show ownership or possession, and for other special uses. (Turn to 402.1-403.4 in *Write Source 2000* for specific explanations and more examples.)

EXAMPLES

To Form Contractions:
isn't (is + not)   **we're (we + are)**

To Form Singular Possessives:
Carey's shoes   **my aunt's sunflower book**

To Form Plural Possessives:
the teachers' meeting   **the women's department**

To Show Shared Possession:
Tim and Janna's cat   **the girls' volleyball**

Directions Add apostrophes as needed in the following sentences. The first sentence has been done for you.

1. Tamara's brother Theo rode her bike and didn't put it away.

2. Katy and Matties mural shows our towns most well-known sights.

3. Ben has three beagles, and you should see those dogs ears when a siren sounds.

4. Tony said he would take everybodys books back to the library but he couldnt do it until Friday.

5. We have to learn all the planets names and their distances from the sun.

6. Jill cant go to the movies because today is her parents anniversary.

7. Our teachers favorite book is *Old Possums Book of Practical Cats.*

8. I promised to take care of Lee McLeans cats while shes on vacation.

All Write pp. 325-326

| Directions | In the story below, put a line through each underlined word that has an apostrophe error. Then correct the error. The first underlined word has been checked and corrected for you. Hint: An additional five underlined words contain apostrophe errors. |

1 William Tell was a hero who lived in Switzerland ~~hundred's~~ *hundreds* of years

2 ago. <u>William's</u> courage and his ability as an archer were widely known. He

3 often spoke out against the cruel emperor and ignored the <u>man's</u> orders.

4 One day, the <u>emperors'</u> patience ran out, and he had William jailed.

5 "Since <u>youre</u> such a brave man and a great marksman," the emperor

6 said, "<u>I'll</u> give you a chance to win your freedom. If you can shoot an apple

7 off your young <u>sons</u> head, <u>you'll</u> be free."

8 Of course, William refused. But the emperor said that if William

9 <u>wouldn't</u> take the challenge, both he and his son would be killed.

10 The whole town held <u>its</u> breath as <u>Williams</u> son stood against a tree

11 and William took aim at the apple. When the arrow pinned the apple to the

12 tree, the <u>people's</u> cheers could be heard for miles. The emperor asked

13 William why he had arrived with two <u>arrows'</u> in his belt, one of which

14 remained there.

15 "If the first arrow had touched my <u>son's</u> head," said William Tell, "the

16 second would have pierced your heart."

Apostrophes 2

The possessive of most singular nouns is formed by adding an apostrophe and *s*. (Turn to 403.2 in *Write Source 2000* for more information.)

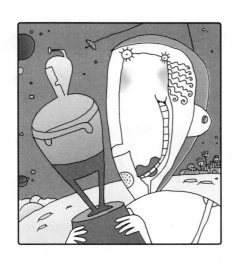

EXAMPLES

Susan's **trophy is at my house.**
(The trophy belongs to Susan.)

I changed the *story's* **ending.**
(The ending belongs to the story.)

Directions   **Use the singular possessive form of each of the following words in a sentence. (Use your own paper if you need more room.)**

1. clock _____

_____

2. friend _____

_____

3. monkey _____

_____

4. _____ (name of a favorite character in a book or story)

_____

_____

5. _____ (name of a favorite movie or sports star) _____

_____

_____

All Write p. 325

Apostrophes 3

The possessive of a plural noun that ends in *s* is formed by adding an apostrophe. (Turn to 403.3 in *Write Source 2000* for more information.)

EXAMPLES

The *stories'* endings were exactly the same.
(The endings belong to the stories.)

Jamila went to the *Greens'* house.
(The house belongs to the Greens.)

Directions Use the plural possessive form of each of the following words in a sentence. (Use your own paper if you need more room.)

1. trees _____

_____

2. Smiths _____

_____

3. bugs _____

_____

4. _____ (name of a favorite sports team) _____

_____

_____

5. _____ (name of a family you know) _____

_____

_____

_____

Italics and Quotation Marks

The titles of longer pieces of writing (books, magazines, albums, etc.) are italicized, while the titles of shorter pieces (short stories, articles, songs, etc.) are placed in quotation marks. (Turn to 400.3 and 401.3 in *Write Source 2000* to review the rules about punctuating titles.)

EXAMPLES

Galactic Soup is my favorite book on the universe.
(The book title is underlined to show italics.)

"Another Time" received two Grammy awards.
(The song title is placed in quotation marks.)

Directions In this exercise, add underlining (to show italics) and quotation marks. The first sentence has been done for you.

1. Were you watching television on July 4, 1997, when the Pathfinder spacecraft landed on Mars?

2. The Pathfinder's Web page on the Internet got more than 500 million hits by people interested in the mission.

3. A few months before the Pathfinder mission, I read an article in USA Today titled Time for the Leap to Mars.

4. Then I read an article in Discover magazine called The Ultimate Suburb about the possibility of living on Mars.

5. I also read a chapter in The Martian Odyssey called The Red Rock Cafe.

All Write pp. 323 and 327

6. The popularity of movies like Star Trek shows that lots of people enjoy science fiction.

7. In 1938, a radio play called War of the Worlds had people believing that Martians had landed in New Jersey.

8. Martians Go Home was a 1990 movie about Martians who come to Earth to cause trouble.

9. I enjoyed the short story about aliens called Playing for Keeps, and I liked the song Galactic Beats from the Music of the Galaxies CD.

10. I am waiting for the morning when I pick up the Houston Chronicle and read an article entitled Life Found on Distant Star. Won't that be something?

Next Step What good-news headlines would you like to see in the newspaper? Think about it and then write a sentence containing three headlines that would make your day. Use quotation marks correctly.

Punctuation Review 1

Directions   Add missing commas and end punctuation to the following passage. Also add capital letters as necessary. The first sentence has been corrected for you. (Turn to 387.1-403.4.)

1   Did you know that Ellis Island was the chief immigration station

2   for the ~~u~~nited ~~s~~tates between 1892 and 1954. in fact nearly 15 000 000

3   people entered the United States through Ellis Island, in the early

4   years the majority of the immigrants came from European countries,

5   such as Great Britain, Ireland Italy Russia and Germany.

6   Ellis Island nicknamed "Heartbreak Island" stood between the

7   immigrants and the new country In a huge inspection room with iron

8   dividers the newcomers were examined by two doctors if the first

9   doctor spotted an obvious physical mental or social problem he put a

10 chalk mark on the person's right shoulder the second doctor looked for

11 diseases and infections have you ever heard of trachoma it is a serious

12 eye disease the second doctor would look for

13   Each immigrant was then questioned every family worried that a

14 family member would be rejected and he or she would have to return

15 home what a horrible thing to have happen most immigrants passed

16 through Ellis Island in about a day but some people had to wait as

17 long as three days

All Write pp. 311-327

18   California has the most new immigrants with New York, Florida,

19   Texas, New Jersey and Illinois following behind Europe is no longer

20   the largest source of immigrants the top six countries for U.S.

21   immigrants in 1995 were Mexico the Philippines Vietnam the

22   Dominican Republic China and India they represented well over a third

23   (40.4 percent) of the total immigrants in that year

Next Step Some people know a little about their family history, and some people know a lot—but everyone knows something. Write a paragraph that tells something interesting about your family history.

Punctuation Review 2

There are times when writers need more than commas and end marks to keep their writing clear. In such cases, they use semicolons, colons, dashes, or hyphens.

To complete the activity below, remember that . . .

semicolons are used before conjunctive adverbs such as "however," and to join two independent clauses.

colons are used to introduce a list or to introduce a formal quotation.

dashes are used to show a sudden break in a sentence.

hyphens are used to join two words.

| **Directions** | Punctuate the following sentences correctly. The first sentence has been done for you. (Turn to 387.1 - 403.4.) |

1. There are four foods I don't like:ₐoysters, liver, fish, and peas.

2. I'm in the mood for a large six topping pizza.

3. My dog is the cutest pet in the world she is all fluffy and white with a black patch around one eye.

4. I wanted to name my dog Madonna however, I was overruled by my mother, who named her Helga.

5. Someone should invent self polishing shoes.

6. The teacher gave us another five paragraph assignment.

7. I know what I want for a present new downhill skis.

8. When I asked my dad if I could go to a movie, I got the usual response "Not on a school night."

9. I pleaded with my dad actually I begged but he wouldn't change his mind.

All Write pp. 311-327

Directions   Carefully read the paragraph below, paying special attention to the underlined words. Put a line through any word that contains an apostrophe error and write the correct form above it. The first two underlined words have been checked for you. Hint: Five of the underlined words (including the one corrected for you) contain apostrophe errors.

When I was little, I used to bake cookies at my grandmother's house all the time. My favorite kind was chocolate chip, but we also baked a lot of peanut-butter cookies. They were my ~~grandpas'~~ *grandpa's* favorite. Whenever it rained, my grandmother would call over to my house and say, "Looks like it's a good day for baking." I'd put on my raincoat, borrow my brothers' bike, and ride over to my grandparents' house. (My bikes' tires always seemed to be flat.) Once there, I'd immediately turn on the oven and keep checking it's temperature while Grandma cracked the eggs. Grandpas' eyes looked a little disappointed when he saw we were making chocolate-chip cookies. Maybe someday I'll bake all of my relatives' favorite cookies.

Next Step   Write a paragraph about a pleasant memory of a grandparent or some other adult. (Use the paragraph above as a model.) Before you share your results with a classmate, check your writing for punctuation errors.

Punctuation Review 3

Directions Proofread the paragraphs below. Draw a line through any mark of punctuation or capital letter that is used incorrectly; add any needed punctuation or capital letters. The first two errors have been corrected for you. (Turn to 387.1 - 403.4.)

1   Imagine yourself sitting in your living room watching TV.

2   Before you can turn your head oil starts gushing through the

3   windows. Pretty soon your whole house is covered with oil. In

4   addition, black sticky oil is all over you. Its in your mouth in your

5   ears, and in your hair. You can't breathe, without getting it in your

6   nose, and theres no clean place in the house where you can go to get

7   away from the stuff

8   This is just what happened in 1989 to the fish birds and other

9   animals that call Alaska their home. An Oil Tanker called the Exxon

10   valdez hit a reef in Prince William Sound. The ships' side had a huge

11   hole ripped in it and the oil inside began spilling out. By the time the

12   spill was stopped: 10 million gallons of crude oil had escaped into the

13   ocean.

14   The massive oil slick then headed for shore fish were poisoned,

15   and seals were left with nothing to eat. Birds who tried to fish for

16   food were covered with terrible black guck. They couldn't preen

17   themselves clean and they couldn't fly to clean water. Even if the birds

18   could have gotten to clean water it wouldn't have done them any good,

All Write pp. 311-327

19 oil doesnt just rinse off. Scientists figured it would take a billion

20 dollars to clean up the oil spill, but now some think, the affected area

21 will never return to normal. The cost's are so high that a portion of

22 the mess will probably just be forgotten and left there.

23   Unfortunately the wildlife may never be able to live again along

24 the affected shoreline

Directions   Work with a classmate, comparing your work before you turn it in. Discuss any differences, and look up your questions in the punctuation section of your handbook.

Next Step Write a descriptive paragraph about the oil spill from a seal's point of view. Here's a possible starting point:
I was basking on the beach when all of a sudden . . .

Mixed Review

Directions   The following paragraphs are missing many types of punctuation: periods, commas, a colon, hyphens, quotation marks, an apostrophe, and italics. Proofread the article carefully, adding the missing punctuation and any necessary capital letters. Double-check your work. *Note:* The actual name of the group in this activity—Boys Choir of Harlem—doesn't need an apostrophe. (Turn to 387.1 - 403.4.)

1   One of the most famous choirs in the United States is probably

2   the Boys Choir of Harlem it was awarded the National Medal of The

3   Arts by President Clinton in 1996 organized as a small boys' choir in

4   the basement of a church the world famous Boys Choir of Harlem now

5   gives 125 performances around the world each year.

6   The genius behind the choir is Dr Walter Turnbull a master

7   teacher and mentor Turnbull has been the choir director for its entire

8   lifetime and he has set high standards for each of the 40 boys in the

9   choir. In the book Lift Every Voice that he co-authored with Howard

10   Manly, he says set goals and complete them the combination of talent,

11   discipline and hard work is unbeatable."

12   The choir sings a variety of music classical modern gospel and

13   jazz more than 2 0 0 0 boys audition for the choir each year one

14   hundred sing in the choir and another hundred are in training for a

15   year and a half Turnbull also runs a school the Choir Academy

All Write pp. 311-327

16   The choir has recorded many CDs such as Christmas with the

17   Boys Choir of Harlem. This CD includes the traditional favorites Silent

18   Night and Little Drummer Boy these young men are multitalented

19   they might begin the evening with Bach and end with a self styled

20   rap people are surprised to learn that we do more than just gospel

21   says Turnbull we do all kinds of music.

Next Step Write a paragraph in which you describe an experience you have had as a singer or performer—in school, at home, or on the playground. When you have finished, exchange papers with a classmate and proofread each other's papers for punctuation errors.

Capitalization 1

You already know that you must capitalize the first word in a sentence. You also know about capitalizing the specific names of people and places. But there are additional rules for capitalization that you should know. For example, you must capitalize names of languages, races, nationalities, and religions. You must also capitalize the names of historical events and organizations. (Turn to 404.1-407.3 in *Write Source 2000* for more information about capitalization.)

Directions   In the following sentences, find the words that should be capitalized. Cross out the lowercase letters and write capital letters above them where needed. The first sentence has been done for you.

1. Rock and roll music came on the scene in the mid to late 1950's in
   places like ~~n~~ew ~~y~~ork ~~c~~ity; ~~k~~ingston, ~~j~~amaica; and ~~l~~iverpool, ~~e~~ngland.

2. Early rock and roll musicians such as elvis presley and little richard
   became international stars.

3. They influenced the next generations of musicians—including
   bruce springsteen and the rolling stones—throughout the United States
   and across the atlantic.

4. On the shores of lake erie in downtown cleveland, ohio, at 1040 east
   ninth street, there's an interesting tourist attraction: the rock and roll hall of
   fame and museum.

5. It opened in september of 1995 and was designed by world-famous architect
   i. m. pei, who also redesigned the louvre museum in paris, france.

All Write pp. 328-332

6. The ahmet m. ertegus exhibit hall, the museum's main hall, is named after the son of the turkish ambassador to the united states who was the cofounder of atlantic records in 1947.

7. The "legends of rock" exhibit features such famous performers as the beatles, michael jackson, tina turner, and aerosmith.

8. A 25,000-song database jukebox plays everything from chuck berry's "maybellene" to led zeppelin's "stairway to heaven."

9. On saturday, july 11, 1998, a. j. hammer hosted a presentation called "rock across america."

10. The museum has an educational office that publishes *backbeat* magazine (spring, summer, fall, and winter issues) for teachers.

11. *Backbeat* has a regular column called "quarter notes" and articles such as "rock and roll goes to the symphony" and "teachers make good rockers."

12. Instead of history 101 or some kind of ancient history course, wouldn't you like to take a course at the museum this summer with a title like "the times they are a-changing"?

Next Step Write a paragraph about your favorite musician (or musical group). Answer the following types of questions in your writing: Why do you like this musician? What are your favorite songs? Have you ever seen the person or group perform?

Capitalization 2

Directions   The following paragraphs have capital letters only at the beginnings of sentences. Supply all of the other capital letters that are needed. (Turn to 404.1 - 407.3 in *Write Source 2000* for help.) The first sentence has been done for you.

1   In 1803, the ~~u.s.~~ US S̶enate approved an incredible deal. It approved a

2   treaty that allowed the united states to buy the enormous louisiana

3   territory for 15 million dollars from france. Only 22 years had passed since

4   the revolutionary war. The u.s. constitution was only 16 years old. The

5   country was young—and small—compared to today.

6   The louisiana purchase, as it was called, came as a surprise. All or

7   parts of this territory had been traded among the french, spanish, and

8   english for a hundred years. The territory had been home to countless native

9   american people for thousands of years. Through his minister of foreign

10   affairs, napoleon, the emperor of france, made a deal with the americans for

11   this territory.

12   Take a look at what was included in the 15 million-dollar purchase

13   price: the present-day states of missouri, arkansas, iowa, minnesota west of

14   the mississippi river, north dakota, south dakota, nebraska, oklahoma, most

15   of kansas, montana, wyoming, colorado east of the rocky mountains, and the

16   part of louisiana that is west of the mississippi. The city of new orleans

17   was also thrown in. For little more than 1 million dollars per state, the

18   united states suddenly doubled in size!

All Write pp. 328-332

19   President thomas jefferson planned an expedition into the territory

20   after reading a book in 1802 called *voyages from montreal.* Americans

21   knew little about the interior of north america. Jefferson hoped someone

22   would discover the northwest passage—a chain of lakes and rivers that

23   people thought must connect the atlantic ocean to the pacific ocean.

24   Jefferson also wanted to find a route for the pioneers who would be moving

25   to the west.

26   Captain meriweather lewis and lieutenant william clark led the

27   expedition. With 48 men they left st. louis, moved up the missouri river to

28   north dakota, and then headed west, down the columbia river to what is

29   now astoria, oregon. During their second season, they had the help of a

30   shoshone guide named sakajawea.

31   The lewis and clark expedition never found the northwest passage

32   (there isn't one), and they did not travel the route that became the oregon

33   trail. They did, however, learn a great deal about the geography and the

34   plant and animal life of the american west and midwest. They established

35   peaceful relations, for the most part, with the native americans they met.

36   When they came back from their 8,000-mile, two-and-a-half-year journey,

37   they were greeted as true american heroes.

Next Step Look at the time line in your handbook and find a topic that you know about or can find in your social studies text. Write a paragraph that explains why this event was important enough to include in a time line.

Capitalization and Abbreviations

When a sculptor creates a face out of a lump of clay, close attention is paid to every detail. The shape of the face must be carefully molded, and each of the face's features must be sculpted in just the right way. Writers are a lot like sculptors since they also must pay close attention to every detail. This includes carefully looking over a final draft, making sure every capital letter is in its proper place and every abbreviation is correctly written. (Turn to 404.1 - 407.3 and 409.4 - 409.6 in *Write Source 2000* for the rules about using capital letters and abbreviations.)

Directions   Carefully read each sentence below. Put a line through any word or letter that is capitalized or abbreviated incorrectly. Make corrections above each mistake. The first sentence has been done for you.

Hint: Go through the activity once and fix everything you're sure about. Then use your handbook to help you with the tougher spots.

1.   M G   S   B
     ~~m~~r. ~~g~~lick bought a ~~s~~aint ~~b~~ernard puppy.

2.   he gave the puppy to ms. plumpcheeks, who lived on mississippi street.

3.   Ms. Plumpcheeks told Mr. Glick that her Mother likes puppies, too.

4.   They decided to go visit her mother in the South.

5.   They took the puppy, which they had named barrelneck, and headed for

     georgia.

6.   mother plumpcheeks kissed Barrelneck and gave him some Spaghetti and

     Meatballs.

7.   "mother," cried Ms. Plumpcheeks, "spaghetti is not good for Dogs!"

8.   "sure it is," said Mother plumpcheeks. "I eat it all the time."

All Write pp. 328-332, 335-336

9. Mr. Glick told Ms. Plumpcheeks that he liked her funny Mother.

10. They decided to take Barrelneck to disney world in Fl.

11. the man selling Disney World Tickets told them that rides weren't good for dogs.

12. "Yes they are," said Mother Plumpcheeks. "I go on rides all the time."

13. Barrelneck and Mother Plumpcheeks rode a Roller Coaster.

14. Later Barrelneck began reading a book called *dog day afternoon.*

15. people thought it was strange to see a dog reading a Novel.

16. "he can't read History books," said Mr. Glick, "Because he never eats his vegetables."

17. Then Mr. Glick, Ms. Plumpcheeks, Mother Plumpcheeks, and Barrelneck went swimming in the Atlantic ocean.

18. A man named Samuel Smart, m.d., told Mr. Glick that swimming wasn't good for dogs.

19. "i know it's so because I graduated from harvard university," said Dr. Smart.

20. They all told Dr. Samuel Smart to go back to his office.

21. Traveling North on their way home, they planned trips to other parts of the U.S.

Next Step On your own paper continue the story of Mr. Glick, Barrelneck, and Ms. Plumpcheeks at a destination of your choice. Then exchange papers with a classmate and check each other's use of capitalization and abbreviations.

Plurals

To form the plural of most nouns you add an "s" or an "es" to the singular. But there are a few exceptions that you need to know. For example, the plural of some compound nouns is formed by adding *s* or *es* to the main word in the compound—as in *brothers-in-law*. Review all of the rules for forming plurals in the handbook before you begin the activity below. (Turn to 408.1-409.3 in *Write Source 2000* for the rules and more examples of plurals.)

| **Directions** | Write the plural form for each of the following singular nouns. The first one has been done for you. |

1. armful   *armfuls*

2. ratio

3. potato

4. lady

5. leaf

6. shovelful

7. hoof

8. mouse

9. CD

10. passerby

11. laboratory

12. chief

13. hobby

14. rodeo

15. half

16. belief

17. secretary of state

18. elf

19. alto

20. stepsister

21. father-in-law

22. A

23. woman

24. duty

25. 4

26. bus

All Write pp. 333-335

Directions   Rewrite each sentence below, changing the underlined phrase from singular to plural. The first sentence has been done for you.

1. May I have a French fry?

   May I have some French fries?

2. Kelly lost the key.

   _____

3. My cousin has a live turkey.

   _____

4. A man came to our classroom.

   _____

5. Sandy bought a dress.

   _____

6. Keir drank a glassful of milk.

   _____

7. Dara put a knife on the table.

   _____

8. A branch fell on our house.

   _____

9. The deer ate from my hand.

   _____

10. My name has one r.

    _____

Spelling

You can avoid some spelling errors by learning a few basic spelling rules that are explained in your handbook. (Turn to 411.1-411.4 and also review the plurals rules at 408.1-409.3 in *Write Source 2000*.) As you will see, most of these rules deal with adding endings to words.

Directions   **Read the sentences below and select the correctly spelled word to write in the blank. You will be able to make the correct choices by applying either the spelling rules or the plurals rules in the handbook. The first sentence has been done for you.**

1. For my birthday, my mother made two huge (*loafs, loaves*) _____*loaves*_____ of banana bread; each one (*wieghed, weighed*) _____*weighed*_____ about two pounds.

2. As a gift I (*recieved, received*) _____ a beautiful book on (*ancient, anceint*) _____ Egypt.

3. I (*hurryed, hurried*) _____ through my (*nineth, ninth*) _____ piece of banana bread before I opened the book.

4. The (*beginning, begining*) _____ was about Egyptian writing, so I'll give you a little (*sumary, summary*) _____ even if I can't (*truly, truely*) _____ describe it all in so little space.

5. The Egyptians were a very religious people who had many (*preists, priests*) _____ , gods, and (*goddesses, godesses*) _____ that they worshiped.

   All Write pp. 333-335, 344

6. Specially trained people called scribes were the only ones who knew how to read and write the religious (*inscriptions, inscriptiones*) _____ .

7. The Egyptians' method of writing is known as (*heiroglyphics, hieroglyphics*) _____ .

8. The (*earlyest, earliest*) _____ writing was carved on stone, so I don't think they (*worryed, worried*) _____ too much about typographical errors.

9. Hieroglyphics proved (*confuseing, confusing*) _____ to non-Egyptians because they didn't realize that the (*weird-looking, wierd-looking*) _____ marks could be read from left to right, right to left, or top to bottom.

10. In 1799, a (*soldeir, soldier*) _____ who was (*serving, serveing*) _____ in Napoleon's army discovered the Rosetta stone, a stone inscription that had both Greek and hieroglyphic writing on it.

11. By (*refering, referring*) _____ to the Greek script, which could be read, scientists finally broke the code and read hieroglyphics for the first time.

12. Although writing in hieroglyphics was (*neither, niether*) _____ quick nor easy, it was used for more than 3,000 years on public monuments because it was (*decorateive, decorative*) _____ .

Next Step Ideograms are a form of hieroglyphics using pictures to send messages. (The following is a simple ideogram: 👁♡🕐 .) Make up your own ideograms. Exchange some of your best ones with a classmate and see if you can figure out each other's messages.

Numbers

Some numbers should be written as words, and some numbers should be written as numerals. (Turn to "Numbers," 410.1-410.6, in *Write Source 2000* for explanations and examples.)

Serial No.
1 2 3 Four
5 6 Seven 8
0 Nine

Directions   In the sentences below, all of the numbers are written as words. Find the number words that should be written as numerals and change them. The first sentence has been done for you.

1. Sally's brothers are ~~twelve~~, ~~fourteen~~, and ~~fifteen~~.
   12   *14*   *15*

2. We have to read chapters one and two by March five.

3. Chapter two starts on page thirty-two.

4. Twenty-one students have spent a total of two hundred and six hours doing volunteer work.

5. Jeremy has saved forty-two dollars so far.

6. Jon got three books from the library that are due on July sixteen.

7. My sister has read eighteen two hundred-page books.

8. Mexico City has a population of nearly twenty-five million.

9. I got this paperback on sale for two dollars and fifty cents.

10. The library opens at eight-thirty.

11. The players on his team range from ages nine to eleven.

Directions Write a sentence using each pair of numbers described below. Your sentences can be serious or silly. The first sentence has been done for you.

1. a time of day and a day of the month

   The party is at Tron's house at 12:00 noon on May 2.

   _____

2. an amount of money and a percentage

   _____

   _____

3. a street address and a highway number

   _____

   _____

4. the number of students in your class and a percentage

   _____

   _____

5. a date in history and a number in the millions

   _____

   _____

Next Step Write two sentences that use numbers correctly. Each of your sentences should include at least one number written as a word and at least one number written as a numeral. (If you need ideas, look around at the people and things in your classroom.)

Using the Right Word 1

The words you use are like the clothes you wear—they must fit the occasion. Certain words and expressions you use with your friends are not acceptable in more formal settings. Your teachers, for example, expect you to use language that is appropriate for the classroom. Your teachers also expect you to use language correctly in your writing.

All language learners must focus a good deal of their attention on errors in usage. These errors are commonly made when one word is confused with another. (*Good* is used instead of *well; there* is used instead of *their* or *they're.*) Whenever you review your writing, pay close attention to the pairs or sets of words that often confuse you. Also make sure to refer to "Using the Right Word" in your handbook whenever you have a usage question. (Turn to 419.1-433.5 in *Write Source 2000* for this information.)

Directions	Read the following story. If an underlined word is incorrect, cross it out and write the correct form above it. If the underlined word is correct, leave it alone. The first error has been corrected for you.

1   A few months ago, my mother read a book called *Diet for a Small*

2   *Planet.* The book said it was better to eat less meat and more vegetables.

                    already

3   Mom was ~~all ready~~ a vegetarian (someone who doesn't eat meat), and she

4   wanted the rest of the family to <u>chose</u> the same <u>course</u>. Since Mom did

5   most of the cooking, we <u>new</u> we had to choose between going vegetarian or

6   starving <u>altogether</u>.

7   In order to <u>learn</u> us how to appreciate vegetables, Mom said we'd start

8   a windowsill garden. We all went to the store to <u>by</u> supplies.

9   "Let's grow beans first," said Mom, "because they have <u>alot</u> of protein."

10   "That's a <u>capitol</u> idea," replied Dad. "Beans grow quickly, so we won't

11   have to <u>wait</u> for weeks to get a sprout."

All Write pp. 345-360

12   We planted a variety of seeds. I was <u>aloud</u> to start <u>an</u> tomato plant of

13   my own, <u>too</u>. It was my job <u>too</u> keep the plants watered. I had to water the

14   soil until the <u>wholes</u> on the bottom of the pots started to leak. That's how

15   we <u>new</u> if the plants had enough water. We <u>set</u> the pots next to the sliding

16   glass door in the kitchen because <u>a lot</u> of sunlight comes <u>threw</u> there.

17   Now all we could do was <u>weight</u>. All three of us checked the pots for

18   sprouts. In less than a <u>weak</u>, everything started to grow <u>accept</u> for the split

19   pea seeds.

20   Now my dad and I really enjoy vegetables. We even grow <u>sum</u> unusual

21   vegetables in the pots in our kitchen and outside in the garden. Yesterday

22   we cooked up some of our own scarlet runner beans (<u>they're</u> poisonous

23   unless cooked). <u>Its</u> fun growing <u>you're</u> own food!

Next Step Use the following pairs or sets of words correctly in sentences
(use one set of words per sentence): *fewer, less; altogether, all together;*
and *it's, its*. Share your results.

Example:
"Visiting the capitol building is a capital idea," said Grandpa.
(The words "capitol" and "capital" are used correctly in this sentence.)

Using the Right Word 2

Your handbook lists many of the words that are commonly misused in writing—*peace, piece; can, may;* and so on. (Turn to 419.1-433.5 in *Write Source 2000* for this information.)

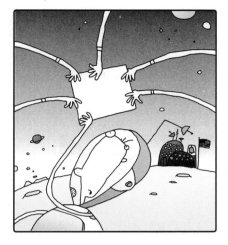

Directions **If the underlined word is incorrect, cross it out and write the correct form above it. Do not change a correct word. The first sentence has been done for you.**

1. Gina's party would be fun, but I was <u>very</u> concerned about Annie and
   personal
   Nathan's ~~personnel~~ problems.

2. My thoughts hadn't <u>aloud</u> me a moment's <u>piece</u>, so I wrote a note to Erin.

3. During the video, in the <u>quite</u> of the classroom, I <u>past</u> my note to Tom.

4. This is where it got <u>quite</u> out of control.

5. Tom thought the note was <u>four</u> Eric and gave it to him.

6. Eric <u>excepted</u> it, <u>red</u> it, and <u>passed</u> it on to show Scott.

7. Scott, <u>who's</u> eyesight must not be very <u>well</u> in the dark, turned it in.

8. Mr. Kline <u>read</u> it and complimented Scott on writing his notes so <u>good</u>!

9. The note read, "Everybody is thinking <u>sew</u> much about Gina's party. Annie
   and Nathan need to get along. I hope <u>sum</u> peace comes <u>vary</u> soon."

10. Mr. K.—apparently with <u>week</u> eyesight—<u>red</u>, "Everybody is thinking about
    Ghana. The animals and native people need help. I hope peace comes soon."

11. I also learned that Mr. K. is <u>vary</u> nice because he leaned over, smiled, and
    said to me, "<u>You're</u> handwriting is improving."

All Write pp. 345-360

Using the Right Word 3

Your handbook lists many of the words that are commonly misused in writing: *bring, take; its, it's;* and so on. (Turn to 419.1-433.5 in *Write Source 2000* for this information.)

Directions **Cross out any underlined word that is incorrect and write the correct form above it. Do not change a word that is correct. The first sentence has been done for you.**

1.   *that*
   Apatosaurus was a dinosaur ~~who~~ lived about 150 million years ago.

2. Herds of apatosaurs traveled across planes, living on leaves and grasses.

3. Ginkgo trees were there principal source of food.

4. Apatosaurs may have been very quite, like giraffes.

5. A healthy apatosaur's wait was about 30 tons.

6. It took 1,000 pounds of food every day to satisfy it's hunger.

7. Scientists right books about dinosaurs, yet no one is quiet sure what they were like.

8. Scientists must infer information about dinosaurs from there fossils.

9. One thing they don't know about is the apatosaur's color, although it may have been gray.

10. Its a mystery, to, whether they could run good or just plod along clumsily.

11. We'll probably never piece together enough information to answer all of our questions about apatosaurs ore the other kinds of dinosaurs.

Next Step Use the following pairs or sets of words correctly in sentences (use one set of words per sentence): *accept, except; allowed, aloud; farther, further;* and *moral, morale.* Share your results.

Using the Right Word 4

Your handbook lists many of the words that are commonly misused in writing: *chose, choose; stationary, stationery;* and so on. (Turn to 419.1-433.5 in *Write Source 2000* for this information.)

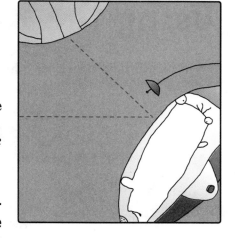

Directions If an underlined word is incorrect, cross it out and write the correct form above it. Do not change a correct word. The first sentence has been done for you.

There

1. ~~Their~~ is only one class that I do not like in school, and that is gym class.

2. <u>Four</u> the kids who run and jump <u>good</u>, I'm sure <u>its</u> great.

3. But for nonathletic types like me, <u>its</u> torture.

4. <u>Beside</u> looking silly in a gym uniform, I'm always picked last when <u>it's</u> time to <u>chose</u> teams.

5. The other kids never <u>leave</u> me have the ball when we play basketball.

6. They say I'm <u>to</u> short <u>to</u> shoot a basket.

7. During softball, I can never hit the ball hard enough to get <u>passed</u> first base.

8. Of <u>coarse</u>, the worst part is trying not <u>too</u> look foolish.

9. During tumbling, I can't do a somersault—let alone a <u>stationery</u> headstand.

10. I feel as if <u>their</u> is a <u>led</u> weight dragging behind me during gym class.

11. When I <u>here</u> the teacher blow that <u>medal</u> whistle, I feel like running away.

12. I would <u>by</u> my way out of gym class if the <u>principle</u> would let me.

All Write pp. 345-360

Using the Right Word Review 1

Directions In the following story, draw a line through any word used incorrectly and write the correct form above it. The first one has been corrected for you. (Turn to 419.1-433.5.)

knew

1   When our neighbor's cocker spaniel had puppies, I ~~new~~ I'd get the pick

2   of the hole litter. I narrowed it down to too blonde pups, and then I choose

3   the one with little white paws and freckles. I named him Snooze because

4   their was no puppy that liked too sleep as much as he did. I didn't no much

5   about puppies, but Snooze was only two weaks old when I picked him out,

6   so I had time to learn.

7   My dad and I bought sum wood to build an doghouse. Then my mom

8   said she'd learn me how to train my dog to do tricks. We went to the

9   library and borrowed a book about dog obedience. We red about house-

10 training a dog with compliments (not punishment) and about learning it to

11 heal and sit. Every mourning I'd visit Snooze at my neighbor's house. We

12 past the time getting too know each other. By the time Snooze came home,

13 he all ready knew how to heel and give me his paw to shake.

14   I think we were as deer to him as he was to us. He always raised our

15 moral, and he seamed to watch over us. Accept for all the blonde hair he

16 left on all the furniture, he was an great dog.

 Next Step Use the following pairs of words correctly in sentences (use one set of words per sentence): *sit, set; personal, personnel;* and *threw, through.* Share your results.

Using the Right Word Review 2

| **Directions** | In the following story, draw a line through any word used incorrectly and write the correct form above it. The first one has been corrected for you. (Turn to 419.1-433.5.) |

you're

1   Whether ~~your~~ a dog lover or a cat lover, you won't be board by this

2   brief history of cats. It probably won't surprise anyone to learn that while

3   cats were running wild threw the African jungles, dogs had all ready moved

4   in with humans. An unknown Egyptian tamed a African wild cat, and in

5   know time at all, cats were very popular in ancient Egypt.

6   The cats' principal job was to save the crops by keeping the rat

7   population down. The Egyptians were more then grateful. In fact, the cats

8   did their job so good that they were soon worshiped as gods. Of coarse, as

9   anyone whose ever owned a cat knows, this suited the cats just fine. They

10 always act like there the center of attention.

11   Did you know that when a cat past away in ancient Egypt, you had to

12 show you're grief by shaving off your eyebrows? And the pore soul who

13 killed a cat (even accidentally) was subject to capitol punishment. (These

14 Egyptians were vary serious about they're precious cats!) Despite the fact

15 that Egyptian law aloud no one to bring cats out of Egypt, sailors began too

16 smuggle them out and cell them around the Mediterranean. The courts of

17 Europe were quiet thrilled with their exquisite but useful knew pets.

18   Given this history, is it any wonder that you can't learn a cat to set

19 down or lie its head on your lap . . . unless it wants too? It wood be a insult

20 to it's lofty heritage!

All Write pp. 345-360

Directions	Use the following pairs or sets of words correctly in sentences. (Use both words in a single sentence, or write a separate sentence for each one.)

1. affect, effect

_____

_____

2. annual, biannual

_____

_____

3. beside, besides

_____

_____

4. bring, take

_____

_____

5. fewer, less

_____

_____

6. immigrate, emigrate

_____

_____

Sentence
Activities

The activities in this section cover four important areas: (1) the basic parts, types, and kinds of sentences; (2) methods for writing smooth-reading sentences; (3) common sentence errors; and (4) ways to add variety to sentences. Most activities include a main practice part in which you review, combine, or analyze different sentences. In addition, the **Next Step** activities give you follow-up practice with certain skills.

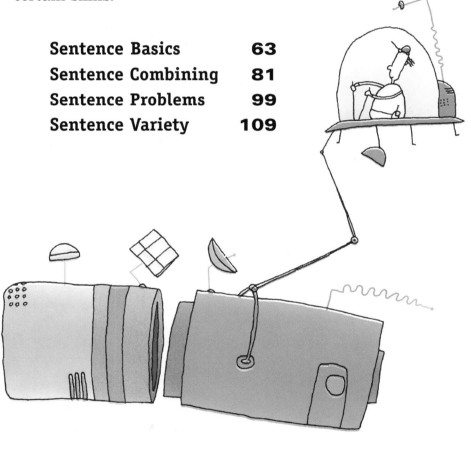

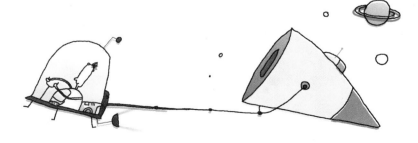

Subjects and Predicates 1

All sentences must have a subject and a predicate (verb) to express a complete thought. The subject is the part of a sentence that is doing something or is being talked about. The **simple subject** is the subject without its modifiers. The predicate is the part of the sentence that says something about the subject or tells what the subject is doing. The **simple predicate** is the predicate (verb) without the words that describe or modify it.

EXAMPLES

Simple Subject:
The ancient <u>Romans</u> counted their citizens regularly.

Simple Predicate:
The ancient Romans <u>counted</u> their citizens regularly.

Directions

In the sentences that follow, underline the simple subject once and the simple predicate twice. *Note:* Helping verbs (*can, could, should, may, have, had,* etc.) are part of the simple predicate. (Turn to 446.3 in *Write Source 2000* for a list of the most common helping verbs.) The first one has been done for you.

1. The U.S. <u>government</u> <u>conducts</u> a census every 10 years.

2. A census is a survey that counts people by age, sex, occupation, and so on.

3. Different surveys collect different types of information.

4. The United States gathers more census information than any other country.

5. No census information can get anyone into trouble with the law.

6. In ancient times, the local folk disliked any census.

7. Higher taxes were often the result of a Roman census.

All Write pp. 368-369

8. The ancient Babylonians collected census information on clay tablets.

9. Fewer than 4 million people lived in the United States at the time of the first census.

10. In 1790, most people lived in 16 states in the eastern part of the United States.

11. Census information determines the number of representatives of each state to the U.S. House of Representatives.

12. In addition, the census gives federal, state, and local governments important information for future planning.

13. Businesses use the census information for their planning as well.

Next Step Suppose you were asked to conduct a survey in your school about athletics, television, or reading habits. With the help of a classmate, write five questions for your survey. Then survey a group of students and compile your results.

Subjects and Predicates 2

All sentences must have a subject and a predicate to express a complete thought. (Turn to *Write Source 2000,* 434.2 - 434.4 and 435.3 - 435.4, for more information.) In the example sentences, the simple subject is underlined once, and the simple predicate is underlined twice.

EXAMPLES

Lasers have hundreds of uses.

Laser light is much brighter than sunlight.

Directions   In the following sentences, underline the simple subject with one line and the simple predicate with two lines. The first sentence has been done for you.

1. In some cases, laser beams are hotter than the sun itself.

2. Light from a laser travels in a narrow line, or beam.

3. In contrast, electric light spreads out into a wide beam.

4. Doctors use lasers in many kinds of surgery.

5. Lasers record music onto compact discs.

6. Lasers in CD players then play the music.

7. In stores, lasers read price tags.

8. Laser beams carry television pictures and telephone conversations.

9. Diamonds are extremely hard.

10. Lasers easily drill holes in diamonds.

   All Write pp. 368-369

Directions	In each sentence below, underline the simple subject with one line and the simple predicate with two lines. The first sentence has been done for you.

1. Often, <u>inventions</u> <u>have</u> very interesting beginnings.

2. The Frisbee began as a pie pan.

3. College students bought some pies at Frisbie Bakery in Connecticut.

4. They ate the pies, of course.

5. Then they played catch with the empty pie pans.

6. The name of the bakery was on the pans.

7. With each toss, the students yelled, "Frisbie!"

8. The game spread to other colleges.

9. A company in California made the first Frisbee.

10. It flew better than a pie pan.

11. In time, people invented many different Frisbee games.

12. Before long, dogs joined in, too.

Next Step Write two sentences about Frisbees. Then underline the simple subjects with one line and the simple predicates with two lines.

Compound Subjects and Predicates

A sentence may have a compound subject, a compound predicate, or both. See the examples below. The compound subjects are underlined with one line, and the compound predicates are underlined with two lines. (Also turn to 435.2, 435.6, and 435.7 in *Write Source 2000* for more information.)

EXAMPLES

Jason and Mason play in the Intergalactic Football League.
(The subject *Jason* and *Mason* is compound.)

Mason plays linebacker and returns punts.
(The predicate *plays* and *returns* is compound.)

Jason and Mason block and tackle for a living.
(The subject and predicate are both compound.)

Directions   Underline each simple subject with one line and each simple predicate with two lines. In each sentence, the subject or predicate may or may not be compound. The first sentence has been done for you.

1. Jim came in and sat down.

2. Molly and I watched a video.

3. Jonathan logged on and checked his e-mail.

4. He got an e-mail from his cousins in Tokyo.

5. Andrew and Hannah wrote about life in Japan.

6. They still play baseball and go to movies.

7. They ride a train, instead of a bus, to school.

8. Hannah reads and writes Japanese.

All Write p. 369

Directions	All of the following sentences have a compound subject, a compound predicate, or both. Underline each simple subject with one line and each simple predicate with two lines. The first sentence has been done for you.

1. Slick <u>roads</u> or heavy <u>traffic</u> sometimes <u><u>makes</u></u> us late for school.

2. The teacher went to the board and started writing.

3. Our neighbors went to the Grand Canyon and hiked for a week.

4. They took pictures and brought back postcards.

5. Shannon and I heard all about their trip.

6. After dinner, Ross and Lindsey do their homework and play computer games.

7. Summer and fall are my favorite times of year.

8. Snow or ice on the roads slows traffic and makes driving dangerous.

9. Earth orbits the sun and rotates on its axis.

10. Neptune and Pluto are farther from the sun and colder than Earth.

11. Tim wrote a science-fiction story and put it on our Web site.

12. Some students in Australia saw his story and liked it.

Next Step Write three sentences that have both a compound subject and a compound predicate. Underline the compound subjects with one line and the compound predicates with two lines.

Prepositional Phrases

A phrase is a group of words that lacks a subject, a predicate, or both. In most cases, a phrase works as a modifier in a sentence. The most common type of phrase is the prepositional phrase. Every prepositional phrase begins with a preposition (*in, at, by, with,* etc.) and ends with the object of the preposition (the nearest noun or pronoun). In between may be words that modify the object of the preposition. Study the examples below and the ones in your handbook for more information. (Turn to 455.1‑455.3 in *Write Source 2000.*)

EXAMPLES

Stephanie plays basketball in her driveway.
(preposition: *in*; object: *driveway*; modifier: *her*)

The ball belongs to Stephanie and me.
(preposition: *to*; compound object: *Stephanie* and *me*)

Directions	Underline the prepositional phrases in the sentences that follow. Circle each preposition. Draw an arrow to each object of a preposition. The first sentence has been done for you. (The number of prepositional phrases is listed in parentheses after each sentence.)

1. How much do you know (about) the game (of) basketball? (2)

2. The game of basketball was invented by Dr. James Naismith in 1891 for indoor use in a YMCA program. (5)

3. For his first game, Naismith used a soccer ball and two peach baskets for goals. (2)

4. Soon basketball was played throughout the United States. (1)

5. Before the modern baskets, net bags were attached to the hoops. (2)

6. Today, millions of fans crowd into arenas for professional games. (3)

All Write p. 398

7. Each team has five players on the floor. (1)

8. The leader of the team on the court is usually the point guard—a quick player with good ball-handling skills. (3)

9. The team also has two forwards; they are taller than the guards and play in the area from the end line to the free throw lane. (3)

10. The tallest player on the team is the center with many important duties, including shot-blocking and rebounding. (2)

11. Basketball is now played in 200 countries worldwide by men and women of all ages. (3)

12. The beauty of basketball is that it can be played in a fancy gym, in a driveway, or on a small city playground. (4)

13. For the fun and excitement of the game, we say thanks, Dr. Naismith, and hip, hip, hooray for basketball! (3)

Next Step Write a paragraph about one of your memorable (or not so memorable) basketball experiences, either as a player or as a spectator. Underline any prepositional phrases you use. Share your results.

Clauses

A clause is a group of words containing a subject and a predicate. An **independent clause** presents a complete thought and can stand alone as a sentence. A **dependent clause** does not present a complete thought and cannot stand alone. A dependent clause must be connected to an independent clause. (Turn to 436.3.)

A dependent clause begins with a subordinating conjunction—*after, although, because, before, when, while,* etc.—or a relative pronoun—*who, whom, whose, which, that,* etc. (Turn to 445.2 and 456.4 in *Write Source 2000* for additional examples of both types of words.)

Note: A sentence containing an independent clause and a dependent clause is called a complex sentence. (Turn to 438.1 in *Write Source 2000* for more information.)

EXAMPLES

Although I don't like writing letters, I love getting them.
("Although I don't like writing letters" is a dependent clause beginning with a subordinating conjunction. "I love getting them" is an independent clause.)

I really enjoy letters that include funny stories.
("I really enjoy letters" is an independent clause. "That include funny stories" is a dependent clause beginning with a relative pronoun.)

Directions   Read the following sentences. Underline each independent clause. Put parentheses ( ) around each dependent clause. The first sentence has been done for you. (One sentence has two dependent clauses.)

1. (Although I always appreciate gifts), I find it hard to write formal thank-you letters.

2. It is especially hard when my mother is on my case.

3. Because this is such a big deal with my mother, I'm trying to understand the issues.

4. My mother is someone who is very set in her ways.

5. If only she counted telephone calls and e-mail, I would be off the hook.

All Write pp. 370 and 372

6. As soon as I open a gift, I like to call the person and say thank you.

7. Formal thank-you notes sound stiff and phony to me, whereas a phone call or an e-mail message seems much more natural.

8. My mother insists on a handwritten thank-you because that is what she has always done.

9. What is so special about writing by hand when there are other ways of accomplishing the same thing?

10. Why do we have telephones and computers if we aren't allowed to use them for everyday things?

11. If a person has e-mail, I have no trouble getting on the computer and keying in a note of thanks.

12. I enjoy technology that allows me to work quickly and efficiently.

13. We will all use 3-D telephones and e-mail to communicate everything when the future comes.

14. Because that happy day has not yet come, you'll have to excuse me.

15. Even though my birthday was two weeks ago, I still haven't gotten around to writing my thank-you note to Uncle Bert.

16. If I would send him an e-mail message, I have no idea what would happen with my mom.

Next Step Write a friendly letter or a thank-you note to someone who deserves to hear from you. Actually send the letter, and experience the good feeling you get from corresponding with someone. Turn to your handbook for guidelines and models.

Types of Sentences 1

There are three basic types of sentences: simple sentences, compound sentences, and complex sentences. See the examples below plus the ones in your handbook. (Turn to 437.3 - 438.1 in *Write Source 2000* for this information.)

EXAMPLES

Simple Sentences:

I dug a huge hole.

(one subject; one verb)

Dad found and bought the perfect tree.

(one subject; compound verb)

Dad and I placed the tree in the hole.

(compound subject; one verb)

Compound Sentence:

I quickly filled in the hole, and Dad gave the tree a good watering.

(two independent clauses joined by a comma plus "and")

Complex Sentence:

After we finished our work, we admired the new tree.

(one dependent clause, "after we finished our work," plus one independent clause, "we admired the new tree")

Directions   Identify each sentence below by writing either *simple, compound,* or *complex* on the blank space. The first sentence has been done for you.

compound   **1.** Forests once covered two-thirds of the earth, but now they cover only one-third of the earth.

_____   **2.** We need forests to survive.

_____   **3.** We breathe in oxygen and give off carbon dioxide.

_____   **4.** Trees are just the opposite because they breathe in carbon dioxide and give off oxygen.

All Write p. 372

_____ **5.** This is a great arrangement for humans, and we should all be grateful to the trees.

_____ **6.** Trees are cut down for houses, paper, fuel, lumber, and other uses.

_____ **7.** If enough trees are cut down, animal species begin to disappear.

_____ **8.** Trees hold the soil in place, and soil erosion is then reduced.

_____ **9.** When the wind blows, trees can serve as effective windbreaks.

_____ **10.** Forests offer valuable shelter for wildlife, and they provide innumerable recreation areas for people.

_____ **11.** Although there are about 20,000 kinds of trees, only 1,000 kinds grow in the United States.

_____ **12.** Each year the average American uses wood products equal to a 100-foot-tall tree.

_____ **13.** People throughout the world eat fruit, nuts, and other tree products.

_____ **14.** The bark of the cinchona tree contains quinine, which doctors use to treat malaria.

_____ **15.** All of us should plant a tree every year so that we can maintain a good supply of beautiful trees.

Next Step *What would your life be like without trees?* Write a paragraph in which you answer this question in detail. Afterward, identify your first four sentences as either "simple," "compound," or "complex." Share your results.

Types of Sentences 2

A compound sentence is made up of two or more simple sentences joined by a coordinating conjunction, by punctuation, or by both. (Turn to 456.4 in *Write Source 2000* for a list of coordinating conjunctions.) The examples below show you how compound sentences can be formed.

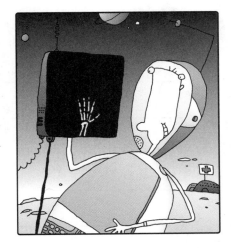

EXAMPLES

The skeleton gives your body shape, but it also protects your vital organs.

(In this compound sentence, a comma and the coordinating conjunction *but* connect the two simple sentences.)

Your body framework is vital to life; learn as much as you can about it.

(In this compound sentence, a semicolon connects the two simple sentences.)

Directions   **Turn each set of simple sentences into a compound sentence using a comma and a coordinating conjunction. For the first three sets of sentences, use the coordinating conjunction in parentheses. The first one has been done for you.**

1. Your skeleton is invisible. It never lets you down. **(yet)**

   Your skeleton is invisible, yet it never lets you down.

2. Without your skeleton, you would be unable to move. Your muscles would have nothing to attach themselves to. **(for)**

3. An adult person has 206 bones. A baby may have as many as 270. **(but)**

    All Write pp. 372 and 399

4. Gradually, some bones in a child's body fuse together. This results in an adult with fewer bones.

    _____

    _____

5. Your skull has 22 bones. Only the lower jaw is movable.

    _____

    _____

6. Your skull bones protect your brain and eyes. The bones in your rib cage protect your heart and lungs.

    _____

    _____

7. The longest bone in the body is the thighbone. It is also the strongest.

    _____

    _____

8. The tiniest bones in the body are the three bones in your middle ear. Without them, you couldn't hear.

    _____

    _____

Next Step List the following names of bones on your paper: *clavicle, sternum, phallanges, patella, tibia,* and *tarsals.* Then write the location of each type of bone next to its name. You may need to study a diagram of a human skeleton. Use this information to write three pairs of simple sentences. Exchange papers with a classmate and try combining the sentence pairs into compound sentences.

Kinds of Sentences 1

There are four kinds of sentences: *declarative, interrogative, imperative,* and *exclamatory.* A declarative sentence makes a statement. An interrogative sentence asks a question. An imperative sentence makes a request or gives a command. An exclamatory sentence communicates strong emotion. To make sure you understand each kind of sentence, study the examples below and the ones in your handbook. (Turn to 438.3 - 438.6 in *Write Source 2000* for this information.)

EXAMPLES

Declarative:
Volcanoes have terrified people throughout history.

Interrogative:
Why are they so terrifying?

Imperative:
Read the following to find out.

Exclamatory:
You'll be amazed!

Directions In the blank before each sentence, write *declarative, interrogative, imperative,* or *exclamatory.* The first sentence has been done for you.

interrogative 1. Where are volcanoes most likely to occur?

_____ 2. Read the following description to find out.

_____ 3. Most volcanoes occur in a rim around the Pacific Ocean called the "ring of fire."

_____ 4. Major eruptions are usually preceded by eruptions of steam and ash.

_____ 5. The initial steam and ash eruptions are sort of like the volcano clearing its throat.

_____ 6. Do you know what happens next?

All Write p. 373

_____ **7.** Bang! The volcano blows its top!

_____ **8.** In other words, the magma erupts through the central and side vents.

_____ **9.** What are some of the major volcanic eruptions throughout history?

_____ **10.** In A.D. 79, Mt. Vesuvius near Pompeii, Italy, erupted and killed about 2,000 fleeing people.

_____ **11.** Volcanoes erupted in Krakatoa (East Indies) in 1883, and more than 36,000 people died.

_____ **12.** In 1902, a volcanic explosion wiped out the entire community of St. Pierre on Martinique in the West Indies.

_____ **13.** The sole survivor was a man who was being held captive in a dungeon.

_____ **14.** That's incredible!

_____ **15.** Is there anything that's good about volcanoes?

_____ **16.** Volcanic ash is very fertile, which is why many people have continued to live in the shadow of volcanoes over the years.

_____ **17.** Check the Internet or a good encyclopedia to find out more about volcanoes.

Next Step Find out more about one of the eruptions mentioned above (or another one). List at least three or four facts that you discover, and then use these facts in a paragraph about your subject. Try to use at least two kinds of sentences in your writing.

Kinds of Sentences 2

All sentences are either declarative, interrogative, imperative, or exclamatory. To understand each kind, study the examples below and the ones in your handbook. (Turn to 438.3 - 438.6 in *Write Source 2000* for this information.)

EXAMPLES

Declarative:
Everyone has a weather story to share.

Interrogative:
What's your story?

Imperative:
Tell me about it.

Exclamatory:
No way, that didn't really happen!

Directions   Write about weather in your part of the country using the four kinds of sentences. Be sure to use correct end punctuation.

Declarative _____

_____

Interrogative _____

_____

Imperative _____

_____

Exclamatory _____

_____

All Write p. 373

Directions

You may never have experienced a tornado or dust storm. Then again, maybe you have! In any case, everyone has had a specific experience with the weather that would make a good story. Think about a time when you were in the middle of a bad storm, watched snow pile up in a blizzard, saw the aftermath of a hurricane or a flood, and so on. Describe that experience in a paragraph of 5-8 sentences. Use at least three kinds of sentences in your description.

_____

_____

_____

_____

_____

_____

_____

_____

_____

_____

_____

_____

_____

_____

Next Step Add an illustration to your paragraph and, as a class, post your work around the classroom.

Sentence Combining with Key Words

When you combine sentences, you make one smoother, more detailed sentence out of two or more short, choppy ones. One basic way to combine shorter sentences is to move a *key word* from one sentence to the other sentence. To see how this is done, study the examples below and the ones in your handbook. (Turn to page 94 in *Write Source 2000* for this information.)

EXAMPLES

Shorter Sentences:
Clyde's sister eats constantly. Clyde's sister is hungry.

Combined Sentence Using an Adjective:
Clyde's <u>hungry</u> sister eats constantly.

Shorter Sentences:
My mom loves coffee in the morning. She grinds it fresh.

Combined Sentence Using a Compound Adjective:
My mom loves <u>fresh-ground</u> coffee in the morning.

Shorter Sentences:
Tasha's dog begs for food at dinner. Tasha's dog slobbers.

Combined Sentence Using a Participle:
Tasha's <u>slobbering</u> dog begs for food at dinner.

Shorter Sentences:
I plan to go on a diet. I will go on the diet tomorrow.

Combined Sentence Using an Adverb:
<u>Tomorrow</u> I plan to go on a diet.

Directions	Combine the following sets of short sentences into longer ones, using the types of key words asked for in parentheses. Underline each key word you use. The first one has been done.

1. Aunt Mae made liver and onions for dinner. She cooked dinner yesterday.
   (adverb)

   Aunt Mae made liver and onions for dinner <u>yesterday</u>.

All Write p. 56

2. I like dogs. I like them when they are small. **(adjective)**

_____

_____

3. The wolves circled the dark cabin. The wolves were howling. **(participle)**

_____

_____

4. During the emergency, we dialed 911. We dialed quickly. **(adverb)**

_____

_____

5. My shoes hurt my feet. My shoes are new. **(adjective)**

_____

_____

6. The baseball fan received the last ticket. The baseball fan smiled. **(participle)**

_____

_____

7. My sister's hair is scary looking. My sister's hair is pink. **(adjective)**

_____

_____

8. Glinda ate a doughnut. It was filled with jelly. **(compound adjective)**

_____

_____

Sentence Combining with a Series of Words or Phrases

The words *and, but, or, nor, for, so,* and *yet* (called *coordinating conjunctions*) are used to connect words, phrases, and clauses in writing. Don't overuse them. You don't want your writing to ramble on and on.

The examples below show you how to combine shorter sentences by using a series of words or phrases. In each case, you will need to use a coordinating conjunction in your combined sentence. (Turn to page 94 in *Write Source 2000* for more examples.)

EXAMPLES

Shorter Sentences:
My skateboard is new.
My skateboard is fast.
It's great for flips.

Combined Sentence Using a Series of Words:
My skateboard is new, fast, and great for flips.

Shorter Sentences:
Sam drinks milk at breakfast.
He drinks milk at lunch.
He drinks milk at dinner.

Combined Sentence Using a Series of Phrases:
Sam drinks milk at breakfast, at lunch, and at dinner.

Directions   Combine the following sets of short sentences into longer ones using the method asked for in parentheses. The first one has been done for you.

1. The new policy seems unfair. The new policy seems impractical. The new policy seems confusing. **(Use a series of words.)**

The new policy seems unfair, impractical, and confusing.

   All Write p. 56

2. The kids built a clubhouse. They created club rules. They made up a secret handshake. (**Use a series of phrases.**)

_____

_____

3. To earn money for her soccer club, Sarah sells magazines. She sells candy. She sells pizzas. (**Use a series of words.**)

_____

_____

4. While dreaming, my dog Molly taps her front paws. While dreaming, she grins broadly. She also wags her tail. (**Use a series of phrases.**)

_____

_____

5. Earning money is important to Landa. Participating in gymnastics is important to her. Painting people's portraits is also important to her. (**Use a series of phrases.**)

_____

_____

6. Andy loves sports and plays hockey. He plays baseball. He plays football. (**Use a series of words.**)

_____

_____

Next Step Pretend to be a mouse and describe some of the places a mouse can go (*in, out, over, under,* etc.). To do this, use eight prepositional phrases in one rambling sentence that begins "The mouse ran . . . ". (See the list of prepositions in your handbook.) Don't forget to use commas to separate your prepositional phrases.

Sentence Combining with Compound Subjects and Verbs

Sentence combining is especially helpful when your writing sounds a little choppy. For example, you can combine sentences by moving a subject, a verb, or a complete idea from one sentence to another sentence. (Turn to pages 95 and 96 in *Write Source 2000* for examples.)

| **Directions** | Combine the following sets of short sentences into longer ones using the methods asked for in parentheses. The first one has been done for you. |

1. Very few Americans owned a car 100 years ago. The Model T Ford changed all that. (**Use a compound sentence.**)

   Very few Americans owned a car 100 years ago, but the Model T Ford

   changed all that.

2. The Model T Ford was developed by Henry Ford. The Model T Ford was nicknamed "Tin Lizzie." (**Use a compound verb.**)

   _____

   _____

3. A crude, boxlike body was used on this odd-looking car. Bicycle wheels were used on this odd-looking car. (**Use a compound subject.**)

   _____

   _____

4. The Tin Lizzie wasn't glamorous. The Tin Lizzie was cheap. (**Use a compound sentence.**)

   _____

   _____

All Write pp. 57-58

5. Ford produced about 10,000 Model T Fords between 1907 and 1908. He sold them for $850 each. (**Use a compound verb.**)

_____

_____

6. Engineers figured out how to make lighter cars. Efficiency experts figured out how to make cars in less time. (**Use a compound sentence.**)

_____

_____

7. Assembly lines cut costs. They gave many people jobs. (**Use a compound verb.**)

_____

_____

8. The Model T was a Ford design. The Model A was a Ford design, too. (**Use a compound subject.**)

_____

_____

9. The car market forced the Ford Corporation to expand. The expansion increased profits. (**Use a compound sentence.**)

_____

_____

10. Ford planned to share company profits with his employees. He wanted to set a minimum wage. (**Use a compound verb.**)

_____

_____

Next Step Write freely for 5 minutes about a memorable car-related experience. Afterward, underline two sets of sentences that could be combined to make them more smooth reading. Combine these sentences on the back of your paper.

Sentence Combining with Phrases

Ideas from short sentences can be combined into longer units of thought by moving a phrase from one sentence to the other. To learn how to combine sentences in this way, study the examples below as well as the examples in your handbook. (Turn to page 95 in *Write Source 2000* for this information.)

EXAMPLES

Shorter Sentences:
The spaghetti sauce tastes gross. It is on the stove.

Combined Sentence Using a Prepositional Phrase:
The spaghetti sauce *on the stove* tastes gross.

Shorter Sentences:
Bruce was actually reading a book. Bruce is a self-proclaimed book hater.

Combined Sentence Using an Appositive Phrase:
Bruce, *a self-proclaimed book hater,* was actually reading a book.

Directions   Combine each pair of simple sentences using the phrase asked for in parentheses. The first one has been done for you.

1. It was April 3, 1999. I got my braces off. **(prepositional phrase)**

_____*On April 3, 1999*_____ , I got my braces off.

2. My first-grade teacher loved to play Simon Says. My first-grade teacher's name was Mr. Simon. **(appositive phrase)**

Mr. Simon, _____ ,

loved to play Simon Says.

3. Johanna won two medals last week. She's a first-rate gymnast. **(appositive phrase)**

Johanna, _____ , won two medals last week.

All Write p. 57

4. Manuel is studying. He's at the library. **(prepositional phrase)**

Manuel is studying _____ .

5. Mike cheerfully volunteered to help his little brother. His little brother
needed help with his math homework. **(prepositional phrase)**

Mike cheerfully volunteered to help his little brother _____

_____ .

6. Todd goes to the movies twice a week. He's the neighborhood movie freak.
(appositive phrase)

Todd, _____ , goes to the movies

twice a week.

Next Step In the space below, write one original sentence naming six
members of your family (aunts, uncles, cousins, grandparents, or pets
may be included) or six people who live in your neighborhood. Use an
appositive phrase for each name (Cheeks, my fuzzy hamster; Libby, my
older sister; . . . are all in my family).

_____

_____

_____

_____

_____

_____

_____

_____

_____

Sentence Combining with Subordinating Conjunctions

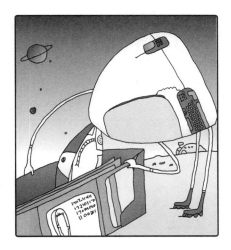

You can combine two simple sentences into a complex sentence using subordinating conjunctions such as *after, although, before,* and *unless.* Note how a subordinating conjunction is used to combine two simple ideas in the following examples. (Turn to page 96 and also 456.4 in *Write Source 2000* for more examples.)

EXAMPLES

Shorter Sentences:
Jon checked his wallet for money. He bought the best-selling thriller.

Combined into a Complex Sentence:
Jon checked his wallet for money before he bought the best-selling thriller.
(The subordinating conjunction *before* connects the two ideas.)

Shorter Sentences:
Katrice studied her math. Amika read a short story in her literature book.

Combined into a Complex Sentence:
While Katrice studied her math, Amika read a short story in her literature book.
(The subordinating conjunction *while* connects the two ideas.)

Note: If the group of words introduced by a subordinating conjunction comes at the beginning of a sentence, a comma is placed after the introductory clause.

Directions Combine the following sets of short sentences into complex sentences. Use the subordinating conjunctions given in parentheses for the first four sentences. The first one has been done for you.

1. The rope-and-wood bridge collapsed. Joe stood and watched. **(as)**

   The rope-and-wood bridge collapsed as Joe stood and watched.

2. The first colonists looked to England for help. It had been their home. **(because)**

   _____

   _____

All Write pp. 58 and 399

3. Maurice filled his bicycle tires with air. He pedaled to the south side of town. **(after)**

_____

_____

4. Jamell settled into his favorite fishing spot. The sun came up. **(as)**

_____

_____

5. Scotty stopped running. He heard the police officer shout.

_____

_____

6. Two feet of snow fell. Reva made it home.

_____

_____

7. You're all set to go to camp. You haven't registered properly.

_____

_____

8. Rosario checked on the two children. She fell asleep.

_____

_____

Next Step Write freely for 5 minutes about what happened yesterday afternoon between the time you were dismissed from your last class and the time you sat down to dinner. Put in as much detail as you can. Then exchange your writing with a classmate. Note two sets of sentences in each other's work that could be combined. When your paper is returned, try connecting the marked sets of sentences as you did above.

Sentence Combining with Relative Pronouns

You can combine two simple sentences into a complex sentence using adjective clauses. An adjective clause is one that begins with a word like *who, which,* or *that* (called *relative pronouns*). Combining ideas with these words will help you cut down on unnecessary repetition in your writing. To learn how this is done, study the examples below as well as the examples in your handbook. (Turn to pages 96 and 444-445 in *Write Source 2000*.)

EXAMPLES

Simple Sentences:
The radio station played unfamiliar songs.
The radio station was geared for an older audience.

Combined into a Complex Sentence:
The radio station, <u>which</u> was geared for an older audience, played unfamiliar songs.

(By combining the two ideas with *which,* the unnecessary repetition of *radio station* is avoided.)

Simple Sentences:
The newspaper gives detailed statistics for major league baseball.
The newspaper is delivered to our school.

Combined into a Complex Sentence:
The newspaper <u>that</u> is delivered to our school gives detailed statistics for major league baseball.

(By combining the two ideas with *that,* the unnecessary repetition of *newspaper* is avoided.)

Directions   Combine the following pairs of simple sentences into one complex sentence. In each case, a relative pronoun, other key words, and punctuation marks have already been put into place. The first one has been done for you.

1. The beady-eyed mail carrier delivers on Wednesdays. The beady-eyed mail carrier is my uncle.

The beady-eyed mail carrier who ___*delivers on Wednesdays*___ is ___*my uncle*___ .

All Write **pp. 58 and 382**

2. The waitress works at the corner cafe. She looks sad and weary.

The waitress who _____ looks

_____ .

3. The pink Cadillac was parked in the driveway. The pink Cadillac convertible was dented by hail.

The pink Cadillac convertible that _____

was dented _____ .

4. The statue stood by the birdbath in the garden. It was stolen.

The statue that _____

was _____ .

5. Pluto is the most distant planet in our solar system. It takes 248 years to orbit the sun.

Pluto, which _____ ,

is _____ .

6. The extreme heat affected the runners. The runners were participating in the conference relays.

The extreme heat _____ who

were _____ .

7. John's half-eaten apple is a Golden Delicious. The apple is now totally brown.

John's half-eaten apple, which is now _____ ,

is _____ .

Next Step Turn to your handbook and find out when you should use "who/which/that." Discuss the results of your research with a classmate.

Sentence Combining with Phrases and Clauses

Using a variety of sentence lengths, and combining shorter thoughts into smooth, longer sentences, can make your writing easier and more interesting to read. (Turn to the sentence-combining section on pages 93 - 96 in *Write Source 2000* for explanations and examples.)

Directions | Combine each pair of simple sentences using the type of phrase asked for in parentheses. The first one has been done for you.

1. For centuries, people have traveled between England and France. They traveled by boat. (**prepositional phrase**)

   For centuries, people have traveled between England and France

   by boat.

2. Nowadays, they can ride a train through the "Chunnel." The Chunnel is a tunnel under the water between England and France. (**appositive phrase**)

   _____

   _____

3. People can take their cars. They take their cars aboard the train. (**prepositional phrase**)

   _____

   _____

4. The Chunnel trip is 31 miles long. It is a half-hour ride across the channel. (**appositive phrase**)

   _____

   _____

All Write pp. 56-58

> **Directions** Combine the following sets of simple sentences into complex sentences using the relative pronouns given in parentheses. *Note:* Use commas in your combined sentences where necessary.

1. The Chunnel runs under the English Channel. The English Channel separates England from the European continent. (**which**)

_____

_____

2. The Chunnel trains are among the fastest in Europe. They travel at speeds of up to 186 miles per hour. (**which**)

_____

_____

3. Europeans have discussed a land crossing to England since the time of Napoleon. Napoleon was emperor of France in the early 1800's. (**who**)

_____

_____

4. London's Chunnel station is named after the town of Waterloo. Napoleon was defeated at Waterloo in June 1815. (**where**)

_____

_____

5. Napoleon was defeated by the Duke of Wellington. Wellington was a British soldier and statesman. (**who**)

_____

_____

> **Next Step** In your class, see who can write the longest complex sentence. Be sure to use relative pronouns and punctuation correctly.

Sentence-Combining Review 1

Directions Combine the following sets of short sentences into single, longer ones. Combine each set using the method asked for in parentheses. (Turn to pages 93 - 96 in *Write Source 2000* for help.) The first one has been done for you.

1. Daisy drank a quart of milk. Then she sat down to dinner. (**Use a subordinating conjunction.**)

   After Daisy drank a quart of milk, she sat down to dinner.

2. Katie goes swimming every day. Josh goes swimming every day. (**Use a compound subject.**)

   _____

3. The snake is long. He is strong. The snake is dangerous. (**Use a series of words.**)

   _____

4. My mom always picked the weeds. They still took over her garden. (**Use a subordinating conjunction.**)

   _____

   _____

5. The hostess took us to our table. She handed us menus. (**Use a compound verb.**)

   _____

   _____

| **Directions** | Combine the following sets of simple sentences and then finish the story on your own paper. Key words and punctuation marks are included in each sentence to help you with your work. The first combined sentence has been done for you. |

1. Rachel's heart was pounding. She stood watching the softball game.

   Rachel's heart was pounding as she stood watching the softball game.

2. This was the third game of the season. Rachel still hadn't gotten to play.

   _____ , and

   _____ .

3. She should have been sitting on the bench. She was too anxious to sit still.

   _____ , but

   _____ .

4. Rachel was small for her age. She had been practicing hard and was eager to help her team win.

   Although _____ ,

   she had _____

   _____ .

5. The fifth inning started. Coach Suarez looked down the bench. He saw Rachel.

   When _____ ,

   Coach Suarez _____ and

   _____ . The coach also saw Sonja

   next to her. He had to decide . . . **(Finish on your own paper.)**

Next Step Exchange stories with a classmate. Check each other's work for shorter sentences that could be combined like those you created above.

Sentence-Combining Review 2

| Directions | Combine the following sets of shorter sentences into single, longer ones. Combine each set using the method asked for in parentheses. (Turn to pages 93 - 96 in *Write Source 2000* for help.) The first one has been done for you. |

1. Breaking an arm or a leg hurts. Spraining a wrist or an ankle is also painful. (**Use a compound sentence.**)

   Breaking an arm or a leg hurts, but spraining a wrist or an ankle is

   also painful.

2. These injuries aren't life threatening, but they are often very painful. These injuries are common. (**Use a key word.**)

   _____

   _____

3. "It's just a sprain," they say. Your ankle swells and turns an ugly purple color. (**Use a subordinating conjunction.**)

   _____

   _____

4. What is a sprain? What causes it to happen? (**Use a compound sentence.**)

   _____

5. Ligaments hold your bones together at the joints. Ligaments are bands of strong tissue. (**Use an appositive phrase.**)

   _____

   _____

All Write pp. 55-58

6. Your shoulders have joints. Your elbows have joints. Your knees have joints. **(Use a series of words.)**

_____

_____

7. You're running at top speed. Suddenly you stop, pivot, jump, and then land with a "Yeow!" **(Use a subordinating conjunction.)**

_____

_____

8. The injury sends you to the floor. It shoots the painful message to your brain. **(Use a relative pronoun.)**

_____

_____

9. Ice decreases the pain. It decreases swelling. It decreases injury to the tissue. **(Use a series of words.)**

_____

_____

10. Reach for an ice pack. Reach for some ice cubes or for a bag of frozen peas if nothing else is available. **(Use a series of phrases.)**

_____

_____

Next Step Make a list of phrases that describe an injury you have had. Then combine the phrases into sentences to summarize your experience.

Sentence Fragments

A sentence must have a subject and a verb, and it must also express a complete thought. A **fragment** occurs when a group of words is missing either a subject or a verb, or it doesn't express a complete thought. At first glance, a sentence fragment may look like an acceptable sentence because it starts with a capital letter and ends with a period (or other end punctuation mark). To learn more about this sentence error, study the examples below as well as the examples in your handbook. (Turn to page 86 in *Write Source 2000*.)

EXAMPLES

Sentence Fragment:
In less than 10 hours.

Complete Sentence:
Jupiter rotates in less than 10 hours.
(A subject and a verb have been added.)

Sentence Fragment:
Has 16 moons.

Complete Sentence:
Jupiter has 16 moons.
(A subject has been added.)

Sentence Fragment:
Jupiter 10 times bigger than Earth.

Complete Sentence:
Jupiter is 10 times bigger than Earth.
(A verb has been added.)

Directions   Write an *F* on the line before each group of words that is a sentence fragment and an *S* before each complete sentence. On your own paper, change the fragments into complete sentences.

_____ **1.** Jupiter is the largest planet.

_____ **2.** Is the fifth planet from the sun.

_____ **3.** Jupiter, made of gas and ice, a huge, red globe.

_____ **4.** Jupiter so large that 1,300 Earths could fit inside it.

_____ **5.** Jupiter is a big ball of hot gas like the sun.

_____ **6.** Could have been a star if it had been a little bigger.

_____ **7.** This ball of hot gas, like a huge, raging storm.

_____ **8.** Has rings around it like Saturn does.

_____ **9.** Jupiter was named after the Roman king of the gods.

All Write p. 50

Directions	Write an *F* on the line before each group of words that is a sentence fragment and an *S* before each complete sentence. On your own paper, change the fragments into complete sentences.

_____ **1.** My favorite kind of TV show.

_____ **2.** I don't have time for television on school nights.

_____ **3.** Story settings in faraway places fascinate me.

_____ **4.** Starships, space missions, and alien races.

_____ **5.** The odd creature was one of the first aliens encountered by the space exploration team.

_____ **6.** Able to compute numbers and call up information.

_____ **7.** Keeps me on the edge of my seat with mystery and suspense.

_____ **8.** Isn't it interesting to think about life in the twenty-first century?

_____ **9.** Despite exploring the galaxy and expanding intelligence.

_____ **10.** A good sci-fi fantasy on TV helps me "space out."

_____ **11.** May be the way you feel, too.

Next Step Suppose a friend calls to tell you an amazing story, but because of noise, you only pick up fragments of the conversation. On your own paper, turn the fragments below into complete sentences that form a story. Compare stories made out of these fragments.

looked out my window . . .   **exploring we saw . . .**
heard strange noises and . . .   **think it was . . .**

Comma Splices and Run-Ons 1

A **comma splice** occurs in writing when two simple sentences are incorrectly joined with a comma. A comma plus a connecting word, an end punctuation mark, or a semicolon should be used between two simple sentences. A **run-on sentence** occurs when two simple sentences are incorrectly joined without punctuation or a connecting word. (Turn to pages 86-87 in *Write Source 2000* for examples.)

| **Directions** | In the groups of words below, place a *CS* in front of each comma splice, an *RO* in front of each run-on sentence, and a *C* in front of each correct sentence. Correct the sentence errors. The first two have been done for you. |

_____*RO*_____ **1.** Mars is the fourth planet from the sun. It is the one you can see most clearly from Earth.

_____*C*_____ **2.** Mars is only one-half the size of Earth.

_____ **3.** Mars shines with red and orange light, it is often called the Red Planet.

_____ **4.** The Romans named Mars after their god of war its red color reminded them of blood and war.

_____ **5.** Mars has seasons like those on Earth its days are also about 24 hours long.

_____ **6.** Mars has two moons called Phobos and Deimos.

_____ **7.** People used to believe that there were people on Mars, they made up stories about Martians.

All Write p. 50

_____ **8.** About a hundred years ago, scientists thought they saw water on Mars.

_____ **9.** In 1964, a spacecraft called *Mariner 4* went to Mars it took a lot of pictures.

_____ **10.** Scientists studied the pictures, they found no signs of life.

_____ **11.** The pictures did show craters like the ones on our moon.

_____ **12.** Someday, astronauts will go to Mars they will live on the planet for a while and check for signs of life.

_____ **13.** They will be able to see if there is any plant life, they can also check for any signs of water.

_____ **14.** Mars is very much colder than Earth, the astronauts will need food and heated suits.

_____ **15.** It will be great to learn more about Mars when astronauts finally do go there!

Next Step Let's say you want to know more about Mars and other planets in our solar system. Certainly you could refer to a book about the planets in your school library. You could also turn to an encyclopedia, your science textbook, or the Internet. But before you refer to any of these sources, check the information on the planets in the "Student Almanac" of your handbook. Write down two facts you learn from the planet charts.

Comma Splices and Run-Ons 2

To become a good writer, you need to learn as much as you can about sentences. You need to read plenty of other writers' sentences, you need to practice writing your own, and you need to acquire a working knowledge of the sentence basics—including a clear understanding of the different types of sentence errors.

| **Directions** | Put an *RO* in front of any run-on sentences that follow, a *CS* in front of any comma splices, and an *S* in front of any complete sentences. (Turn to pages 86-87 in *Write Source 2000* for examples and information about these sentence errors.) |

_____ **1.** Gwendolyn Brooks loves people you can tell that the first time you

meet her.

_____ **2.** I heard her read her poetry in a Chicago bookstore, she drew a

big crowd.

_____ **3.** We had all come to see and hear the famous poet read some of

her poetry I felt like I was in the presence of a living legend.

_____ **4.** I love her poem "We Real Cool," this is a poem about kids playing

pool.

_____ **5.** When Ms. Brooks was reading her poems, she made eye contact

with each of us.

_____ **6.** She looked like she could be anybody's favorite aunt, that day she

wore a navy blue suit and sensible shoes and carried a big black

handbag.

All Write p. 50

_____ **7.** Ms. Brooks was born in Topeka, Kansas a children's magazine published her first poem when she was 13.

_____ **8.** She grew up in Chicago, this city provided the setting for her first book of poems.

_____ **9.** Much of her poetry is about plain, ordinary black people in the central city she writes about survival, change, and hope.

_____ **10.** Ms. Brooks is also a teacher, many colleges and universities have given her honorary degrees.

_____ **11.** She won the Pulitzer Prize for her poetry in 1950 she was the first African-American to win a Pulitzer.

_____ **12.** In her poetry after 1968, Brooks wrote several works for children.

Next Step Review the "Invented Forms of Poetry" in your handbook. Then write an invented poem about the word *success*. You might try writing alphabet poetry, list poetry, or so on.

Sentence Errors Review 1

Run-on sentences, comma splices, and sentence fragments are three of the most common types of sentence errors. One of your most important jobs when you edit is to check your writing for these types of errors. If your sentences aren't clear and correct, readers will have a hard time following your ideas. *Remember: Accurate copy is one of the traits of good writing.* (To review each of these types of sentence errors, turn to pages 86-87 in *Write Source 2000*.)

Directions   Write *RO* in front of any run-on sentences, *CS* in front of any comma splices, and *F* in front of any fragments. The first sentence has been done for you.

_**CS**_   **1.** "Down under" refers to countries that are south of the equator, however, we usually just think of Australia and New Zealand.

_____   **2.** In Australia, January and February are the warmest months, June and July are the coldest ones.

_____   **3.** Australia is the world's smallest continent it is also the sixth-largest country.

_____   **4.** Much of its interior dry and hot.

_____   **5.** About 70 percent of its birds and 90 percent of its snakes are unique to Australia they cannot be found anywhere else in the world.

_____   **6.** Australia is famous for its unusual wildlife, kangaroos, koalas, and wombats are only three of its strange animals.

_____   **7.** The original people of Australia are called Aborigines, they came to Australia from Southeast Asia about 40,000 years ago.

     All Write p. 50

_____ **8.** The first Europeans on the continent, convicts that were brought

over to Australia from England, Scotland, and Ireland in 1788.

_____ **9.** Today's immigrants come from all over the world, the largest

numbers come from Italy and Greece.

_____ **10.** The most sparsely populated continent on earth (except

Antarctica, of course), with only six persons per square mile.

_____ **11.** Australians have many special names for things they also use

many English terms for things.

_____ **12.** Greet you with a friendly "G'day, mate!" morning, noon, or night.

_____ **13.** Drive on the left side of the road.

_____ **14.** Tea is the favorite hot drink English is the official language.

Next Step Study the map of Australia in your handbook. What is its
capital? What seas surround Australia? What are its latitude and
longitude? What are the names of two of its great deserts?
Approximately how far is it from Hawaii? Gather these facts and
combine them into several complete sentences that give the basic
geographic facts about the continent that is "down under."

Sentence Errors Review 2

Sentences have a way of running out of control. Your goal as a writer should be to avoid the errors that lead to "wayword" sentences. Three of the most common types of sentence errors are run-on sentences, comma splices, and sentence fragments. (Turn to pages 86-87 in *Write Source 2000* for explanations and examples.)

| **Directions** | Write *RO* in front of any run-on sentences that follow, *CS* in front of any comma splices, and *F* in front of any sentence fragments. |

_____ **1.** Yesterday, Indra and I hiked into the woods we wanted to have a picnic lunch with a nice crowd of trees.

_____ **2.** Some sandwiches, chips, and pop in a backpack.

_____ **3.** We had to hike 2 1/2 miles to get to shade, the shortest trail in the park was 4 miles.

_____ **4.** It was hot on that trail, we were sweaty, cranky, and red faced.

_____ **5.** Our pop got warm, the sandwiches wilted.

_____ **6.** The woods were raining wood ticks they fell on our hair and climbed inside our clothes.

_____ **7.** Picked ticks out of my hair when we rested.

_____ **8.** Totally grossed me out!

_____ **9.** The ants drove me crazy, Indra called me a wimp.

_____ **10.** Until she got stung by a bee.

Next Step Rewrite this little story in complete sentences on your own paper. What else might have happened on this outing? Add your ideas to continue the story. Make sure to use complete sentences. Share your results.

All Write p. 50

Rambling Sentences

Be careful not to use too many *and*'s, *but*'s, and *so*'s in your own writing. Otherwise, your sentences might ramble on like those of an excited four-year-old. (Turn to "Rambling Sentence" on page 87 in *Write Source 2000* for more information and an example.)

Directions Read the following paragraph aloud. Listen for sentences that seem to go on forever. Correct these sentences by taking out some (but not all) of the *and*'s, *but*'s, and *so*'s. Then fix the punctuation and capitalization as needed. The first few rambling ideas have been corrected for you.

1   We went up to my grandfather's cabin last weekend. It was

2   fantastic. We went fishing on Saturday morning, and I caught a bass

3   off the pier. so Dad said he'd have Mom cook the fish for lunch.

4   Cleaning a fish is kind of gross because you have to cut it open, but

5   Dad did most of that. and then we went swimming at the swimming

6   hole. My brother Tad and I took turns pushing each other out over

7   the water in a tire swing. Tad would push me hard, and I'd jump off

8   into the water, and then he'd yell for me to swim back and push him,

9   and we spent all afternoon swimming and pushing. On Sunday

10 morning, Dad cooked pancakes and thick, crunchy bacon on the old

11 wood-burning stove, and we ate like pigs, and Tad and I wanted to go

12 swimming again, but then we decided to go for a hike instead. We

13 looked for creepy bugs while we were in the woods and we found slugs,

14 centipedes, and caterpillars, but we also caught a few butterflies, but

15 we let them go. We kept a couple of the caterpillars in a jar and

16 looked at them all the way home in the car.

Sentence Expanding

You needn't pack specific facts and details into all of your sentences in a piece of writing. That would be overdoing it. But, it's also true that you will not hold a reader's attention if most of your sentences lack detail. Note the two sentences that follow.

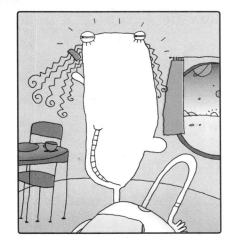

EXAMPLES

John ate the pancakes.

As his sister watched, John ate the stack of pancakes in a single bite.

The basic idea is the same in both sentences: *John ate the pancakes.* However, the second sentence is expanded with more specific detail. It shows when and how John ate the pancakes.

Carefully note below the process of expanding a sentence.

The basic sentence:	**Karlene smiled.**
When did she smile?	*This morning,* **Karlene smiled.**
How did she smile?	**This morning, Karlene smiled** *slyly.*
Why did she smile?	**This morning, Karlene smiled slyly** *as her brother sat in the scrambled eggs.*

Directions   Now you try it. Build the following basic idea into an expanded sentence.

The basic sentence: **Sidney ran.**

When did he run?_____

_____

_____

Where did he run (in what location), or what was his destination?

_____

_____

How did he run? _____

_____

_____

Why did he run? _____

_____

_____

_____

Sentence Expanding Revisited

| **Directions** | Carefully read and evaluate your newly expanded sentence. Decide if it contains too little, too much, or just enough detail. Rewrite it below, trying to make it even better. (Your sentence doesn't have to answer all of the questions asked above.) Share your results with a classmate. |

Revised Expanded Sentence:

Next Step Write three basic ideas that could be starting points for additional expanded sentences. Exchange these ideas with a classmate for more sentence-expanding practice.

Editing for Smoothness and Clarity 1

The effective use of transitions can help you achieve effective organization and smooth-reading sentences in your writing. Transitions are words such as *first, second, soon, finally,* and so on. (Turn to page 106 in *Write Source 2000* for a list of transitions.)

| **Directions** | Use the following transition words to complete the story that follows. Try to use each transition only once. The first one has been done for you. |

and	for example	then
before	for this reason	third
besides	however	throughout
but	in addition	today
finally	on the other hand	to repeat
first	second	

1   Nobody knows when the first dog became a regular at some cave

2   dweller's fire circle. _____*However*_____ , we do know that dogs were the first

3   domesticated animals. _____ recorded history, dogs and people

4   have been buddies. Some dogs have even been considered sacred.

5   _____ , one Native American myth says that even the Creator of

6   the universe was accompanied by a dog. _____ , in this country,

7   the American Kennel Club recognizes 138 different breeds of dogs. On the

8   one hand, you might choose a miniature Chihuahua who weighs under two

9   pounds. _____ , you may prefer a large breed such as

10 a St. Bernard that tips the scales at 200 pounds.

All Write p. 70

11   _____ a dog can do its best, it must be treated kindly and be

12   trained well. _____ it will try hard to please and to serve.

13   _____ , a well-trained dog has many career

14   opportunities. _____ , there are jobs in agriculture.

15   _____ to herding cattle and sheep, dogs cheerfully pull sleds,

16   retrieve objects, hunt, and perform other chores.

17   _____ , there are jobs in law enforcement. _____

18   being natural guardians of their territory and their friends, dogs have an

19   incredible sense of smell that can detect a drop of blood in five quarts of

20   water—a handy skill in this line of work.

21   _____ , there are opportunities for dogs in the social services.

22   Of course, dogs can be trained to help people who are blind to cross streets

23   safely, _____ they can also pick up objects for people in

24   wheelchairs and cheer up people who are depressed.

25   _____ , dogs are natural athletes and entertainers. The

26   circus _____ the TV and movie industry are always looking for a

27   few good dogs to join their ranks. _____ , dogs have many career

28   opportunities, but I'm just happy my dog isn't particularly ambitious.

Next Step Explain a simple process (teaching a dog a new trick, fixing
something, cooking, etc.) in a few sentences. Use transition words such
as *first, second, for example,* and *finally* in your explanation.

Editing for Smoothness and Clarity 2

Transitions or linking words like *finally, however,* and *also* help readers get from one end of your writing to the other in a smooth and logical manner. You have a lot of transitions to choose from to assist your readers along their way. (Turn to page 106 in *Write Source 2000* for a list of transitions.)

(Turn to page 106 in *Write Source 2000* for a list of transitions.)

| **Directions** | Use the following transitions to fill in the blanks below. The first one has been done for you. |

as soon as	finally	before	however
moreover	for instance	in fact	

1   My parents and I get along pretty well. _____*However*_____ , there are

2   certain things we disagree about. _____ , I think

3   my curfew is unreasonably early (8 p.m.). I tried to win them over with

4   many good reasons why I should be able to stay out later. My best friend

5   can stay out until 9 p.m. _____ , everyone I

6   know can stay out later than I can. _____ , I am very responsible

7   and would not get into trouble if I stayed out later. _____ , being

8   able to stay out later would make me more mature. _____

9   I finished my arguments, my father said he'd make my curfew 6:30 p.m. if I

10   didn't stop bugging him about it. _____ , I talked about curfews

11   all the time, but I don't talk about them much these days.

Now, it's your turn to write a story. The transition words have been supplied for you. First, select a subject and put it on the first line below. Then you need to fill in each line with a sentence that fits the transition word and makes sense with your story.

1. One of my favorite things to do on Saturday mornings is _____

_____

_____

2. As soon as _____

_____

3. Then _____

_____

4. Next, _____

_____

5. However, _____

_____

6. For example, _____

_____

7. Finally, _____

_____

Next Step Select five transitions listed in your handbook and use them in a brief paragraph about something funny, surprising, or unusual you've witnessed. Share your results.

Language Activities

Every activity includes a main practice section in which you learn about or review the different parts of speech. Most of the activities include helpful handbook references. In addition, the **Next Step** activities give you follow-up practice with certain skills.

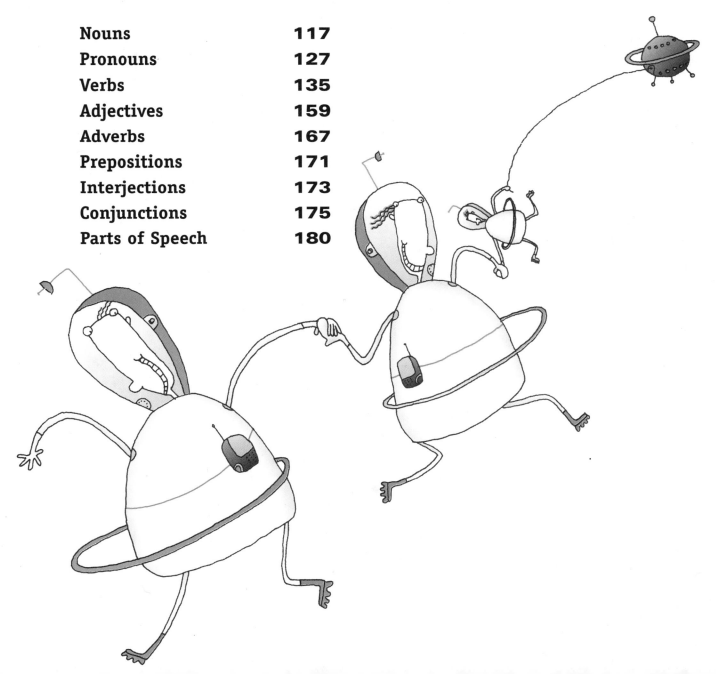

Nouns

Nouns name the people, places, things, or ideas we use in our writing and speaking. Note the nouns (underlined) in the example sentence. (Also turn to 439.1-439.5 in *Write Source 2000* for more examples.)

EXAMPLE

Sally met her new *classmates* in the *hallway*.

Sally names a person, *classmates* names the people who have gathered around her, and *hallway* names the place where they stand. *Sally* is also the subject of the example sentence. (The subject is the part of a sentence that is doing something or about which something is said.)

Directions — Underline the nouns used as simple subjects in the sentences that follow. In the space provided, tell whether each subject (noun) is a *person,* a *place,* a *thing,* or an *idea.* The first one has been done for you.

_____idea_____ **1.** The <u>thought</u> of introducing herself made Sally feel queasy.

_____ **2.** The students stared at the new girl.

_____ **3.** Her nervousness was obvious to everyone.

_____ **4.** The first-hour bell scared Sally.

_____ **5.** The teachers told all the students to get to their first-hour classes.

_____ **6.** Sally had no idea which way to go.

_____ **7.** McKinley School was so much larger than her old school.

_____ **8.** Two girls walked up to Sally, smiled, and offered to help.

_____ **9.** Sally breathed a sigh of relief and thanked the girls.

_____ **10.** Her first-hour classroom was down the hall.

Next Step Write one sentence that includes four nouns, one used as a person, one as a place, one as a thing, and one as an idea.

All Write p. 375

Singular and Plural Nouns

A **singular noun** names one person, place, thing, or idea. A **plural noun** names more than one person, place, thing, or idea. Review the examples below and the examples in your handbook. (Turn to 440.1-440.2 in *Write Source 2000*.)

EXAMPLES

Big celebrations are held every Fourth of July.
(*Celebrations* is a plural noun. *Fourth of July* is a singular noun.)

Many families have a picnic on this day.
(*Families* is a plural noun. *Picnic* and *day* are singular nouns.)

Directions Underline all of the nouns in the sentences that follow. Write *S* above each singular noun and *P* above each plural noun. (The number of nouns in each sentence is given in parentheses.)

1. One <u>celebration</u> was held in the field behind the Bunde Methodist Church. (3)

2. That church is in the country, about three miles from town. (4)

3. There were games and contests with prizes all day. (4)

4. The women from the Ladies Aid Society were competing by having each lady pound a handful of huge spikes into a thick beam. (6)

5. A relay with suitcases for the men always made the people laugh. (4)

6. Another relay for the men entertained everybody. (2)

7. The women watched the men racing to hang laundry on the clotheslines. (4)

8. Shirts hanging by their cuffs looked strange. (2)

Next Step Write five sentences about a Fourth of July you remember. Exchange your sentences with a classmate. Underline and identify each singular and plural noun.

Common and Proper Nouns

A **proper noun** is the name of a specific person, place, thing, or idea. Proper nouns are capitalized. A **common noun** is any noun that does not name a specific person, place, thing, or idea. Common nouns are not capitalized. See the examples below plus the ones in your handbook. (Turn to 439.1 - 439.2 in *Write Source 2000*.)

EXAMPLE

Jim bought a new car from a rental company.
Jim is a proper noun that names a specific person.
The words *car* and *company* are common nouns that name things.

Directions   Underline each noun in the sentences below. Write *C* above each common noun. Write *P* above each proper noun. (The number of nouns in each sentence is given in parentheses.)

1. A company that rents cars must care for them. (2)

2. Each engine receives good care and regular service. (3)

3. Most rental cars stand outdoors, winter and summer. (4)

4. This car, a black station wagon, just received a coat of wax. (5)

5. Jim waxed it yesterday morning, on the last Thursday in July. (4)

6. He has no idea when his car will receive its next coat of wax. (4)

7. Jim drove the car for the first time last week. (4)

8. The car performed well in traffic, especially on the highway. (3)

9. He took his friend Paul Block and his son to Chicago to watch the Cubs play baseball. (6)

10. Once in Skokie, they parked the car and rode the train to Wrigley Field. (4)

All Write p. 375

Directions   In each sentence below, fill in the first blank with a common noun and fill in the second blank with a proper noun. The first sentence has been done for you.

1. If I could buy a _____*car*_____ , I would buy one

made by _____*Porsche*_____ .

2. Alisha plays _____ on a team called

the _____ .

3. Josh got a new _____ ; he named it

_____ .

4. Terri is reading a _____ about the history

of _____ .

5. We watched a _____ called _____ .

6. I had to go to the _____ last _____ .

7. Sasha was born in the _____ of _____ .

8. My favorite _____ is _____ .

9. Michael likes _____ , but only if it's

_____ .

10. Shavon visited _____ , which is located

in _____ .

Next Step Write a poem in which all of the nouns are proper nouns. You can use any of the types of poems in your handbook or a form of your own.

Using Nouns

Nouns are often identified by their use in a sentence. A subject noun is the subject of a sentence. A predicate noun follows a form of the *be* verb and renames the subject. A possessive noun shows ownership or possession. An object noun is used as a direct object, an indirect object, or the object of a preposition. To learn more about the uses of nouns, study the examples below as well as the examples in your handbook. (Turn to 440.5-441.3 in *Write Source 2000*.)

EXAMPLES

Subject Noun:
Hollywood produces many films.

Predicate Noun:
My town is the *capital*.

Possessive Noun:
My *town's* major asset is its people.

Object Noun:
You'll enjoy my *town*.

Directions   Identify the use of the underlined noun in each sentence. Choose one of the following labels: *S* for subject, *P* for predicate noun, *PN* for possessive noun, and *0* for object noun. The first one has been done for you.

1. I have some exciting <u>news</u>.
   0

2. Hollywood has discovered <u>Burlington</u>, my hometown!

3. The film crew arrived to shoot a <u>movie</u>.

4. <u>Ms. Peres</u> and <u>Mr. Snyder</u>, local people from my community, have been hired as assistants.

5. The <u>mayor's</u> face lit up when the announcement was made on local TV.

All Write p. 378

6. Our newspaper is providing full local <u>coverage</u>.

7. Two rising film <u>stars</u> have the lead roles.

8. Two of the "extras" that were hired are <u>Miguel Gomez</u> and <u>Amika Jons</u>.

9. These two people are <u>citizens</u> in our community right now.

10. My <u>life</u> is much more exciting since Hollywood came to town.

11. If I were a Hollywood producer, I'd do a film about <u>animals</u>.

12. This experience is great for <u>Burlington's</u> identity.

13. Four blocks in the center of town will be the primary <u>area</u> for the filming.

14. <u>Dimitri Karas's</u> house is right in the middle of this area.

15. I've never felt so much <u>excitement</u> in our town.

Next Step Write four sentences about your city or town. Each sentence should highlight an interesting, a fun, or an unusual point of interest. Try to label one example for each use of a noun.

Concrete and Abstract Nouns

Nouns can be concrete or abstract. A **concrete noun** names a thing that is physical (can be touched or seen). An **abstract noun** names something you can think about but cannot see or touch. Study the examples that follow as well as the ones in your handbook. (Turn to 439.3 - 439.4 in *Write Source 2000*.)

EXAMPLES

Concrete Nouns:
Andes Mountains   Venus   pickles   dirt

Abstract Nouns:
Buddhism   hope   prejudice

Directions   Read the following passage and underline all the nouns. Above each noun write *C* for concrete or *A* for abstract. The first sentence has been done for you.

1   Have you ever visited the <u>mountains</u>? Theories about how mountains

2   formed are interesting, but I'd rather visit the mountains than study them.

3   My belief is that the mountains are there for enjoyment, and I think that's a

4   good enough reason for their existence. My dream is to visit the Andes

5   Mountains in South America. The most amazing fact about the Andes is

6   that they are the longest chain of mountains in the world. They are a

7   natural wonder that stretches more than 4,500 miles. They spread through-

8   out seven countries from Venezuela to Chile. Someday I would like to climb

9   the Andes, but there is one problem. There is less oxygen in the mountains,

10   and you may end up out of breath. Yet, the people who live in the

All Write p. 375

11 mountains run around effortlessly. They don't know any magic or have

12 special talents. They just develop bigger hearts and lungs so their blood can

13 carry more oxygen to their brains. Despite the breathing problem, I still

14 have a great love for the mountains. At 10,000 feet above the sea, I leave

15 behind my worries and find peace.

Directions Read the opening paragraph on page 149 in *Write Source 2000*. List any concrete nouns and abstract nouns that you find. (Compare lists with a classmate.)

Concrete	**Abstract**
_____	_____
_____	_____
_____	_____
_____	_____
_____	_____
_____	_____
_____	_____
_____	_____
_____	_____

Next Step Where do you find peace? Write a paragraph that describes a place where you feel secure and peaceful. Circle any abstract nouns in your writing.

Specific Nouns

Specific nouns help writers create clear images or word pictures for their readers. Can you recognize award-winning, specific nouns when you see them? To find out, read the two columns of nouns that follow. (Turn to page 135 in *Write Source 2000* for more information about specific nouns.)

EXAMPLES

General Nouns	*Specific Nouns*
shelter	pup tent
poultry	duck
animal	wombat
campground	Camp Runamuck
lake	Mud Lake

Directions	In the sentences below, replace the underlined general nouns with specific nouns. Use nouns that will make the sentences very interesting. The first sentence has been done for you.

1. I want a lot of onions on my ~~sandwich~~ *hamburger* and a lot of sugar in my ~~drink~~ *iced tea*.

2. Our classroom has some <u>fish</u> in a <u>container</u>.

3. Jerry found an <u>animal</u> hiding under his bed at <u>camp</u>.

4. A <u>person</u> rang our doorbell at <u>night</u>.

5. Rosa and I made <u>dessert</u> and then played a <u>game</u>.

6. My uncle raises <u>vegetables</u> and <u>flowers</u>.

7. Sam dived into the <u>water</u> wearing his <u>clothes</u>.

8. A <u>person</u> leaped out of the <u>car</u> and ran into the <u>building</u>.

Next Step Trade papers with a classmate and read each other's sentences. Note the specific nouns your classmate used and how those nouns made his or her sentences different from yours.

All Write p. 92

Directions List at least 10 interesting or important nouns. Look in a dictionary, a thesaurus, or your handbook for award-winning nouns. Also notice appealing nouns as you read books, magazines, and advertisements. How will you know whether or not a noun is "award-winning"? Some suggestions follow:

It might be the *sound* of certain words that attracts you.
(I like the way the words *mozzarella cheese* roll off my tongue.)

Maybe the *feeling* a noun gives you is important.
(The word *willow* gives me a good feeling.)

Then again, maybe a noun has a special meaning for you.
(The word *geranium* has a special meaning for me because every summer my grandmother has these flowers on her porch.)

1. _____

2. _____

3. _____

4. _____

5. _____

6. _____

7. _____

8. _____

9. _____

10. _____

Next Step Share your work with a classmate. Discuss which words you like in each other's list. Use one of your favorite nouns as the starting point for a clustering activity. (Turn to "Clustering" in your handbook for guidelines and a model.)

Pronouns

Pronouns are words used in place of nouns. They allow us to communicate clearly and smoothly. Most of the pronouns we use are personal pronouns (*I, we, they, he, her,* etc.), but there are other types as well. The following sentence reveals the importance of pronouns in our language. (Turn to 441.4 - 445.3 in *Write Source 2000* to find out about all types of pronouns.)

EXAMPLES

Sentence without Pronouns:
Mr. Lee thought that Mr. Lee should write Mr. Lee's name on the board.
(Repeating the noun *Mr. Lee* sounds a little strange.)

Sentence with Pronouns:
Mr. Lee thought that he should write his name on the board.
(Using the pronouns *he* and *his* for *Mr. Lee* makes this sentence smoother and easier to understand.)

Directions	Underline the *personal pronouns* in the following sentences. (The number of personal pronouns in each sentence is given in parentheses.) The first one has been done for you.

1. My husband and I asked our elderly neighbor to plant some trees for us. (4)

2. He dug two ash saplings out of his grove; they had grown there wild. (3)

3. In early spring, he came with them, their roots neatly balled in burlap. (3)

4. I watched as he skillfully planted those trees, his hands knowing exactly what to do. (3)

5. Their branches were full of leaf buds. (1)

6. "When you transplant a tree," he said, "you must leave the taproot as long as possible." (3)

7. With his feet, he firmly tamped down the soil around the roots. (2)

8. As he put his tools away, we asked him in for a cup of coffee. (4)

All Write p. 379

Antecedents

The word that the pronoun replaces is called the *antecedent*. If the antecedent is singular, the pronoun must be singular; if it is plural, the pronoun must be plural. Study the examples below as well as the ones in your handbook. (Turn to page 90, and then also look at 441.4 in *Write Source 2000*.)

EXAMPLES

The players won *(his/their)* **matches.**
(The antecedent *players* is plural, so the pronoun must be plural.)

A soldier may one day become an officer if *(he or she/they)* **is dedicated.**
(The antecedent *soldier* is singular, so the pronoun must be singular.)

Directions Underline the correct pronoun in parentheses. Then draw an arrow to its antecedent. (Use *him or her, his or hers,* etc., when either a male or female could be referred to by the antecedent.)

1. Both magazines offered *(its/their)* customers a good deal.

2. The boss will hire anyone if *(he or she/they)* can serve on weekends.

3. Paula and Rosa brought samples of *(her/their)* winning recipe.

4. The club decided to raise *(its/their)* membership dues.

5. Not everyone should do weight lifting in *(his or her/their)* exercise program. (*Everyone* is a singular antecedent.)

Next Step Write five sentences that include pronouns and antecedents. Exchange papers with a classmate and underline each pronoun. Then draw an arrow to its antecedent just as you did in the sentences above.

Subject and Object Pronouns

Since pronouns substitute for nouns in a sentence, they are used in the same ways. For example, a *subject pronoun* is used as the subject in a sentence. A subject pronoun is also used after a form of the *be* verb (*is, are, was, were,* etc.). An *object pronoun* can be used as the object of a verb or the object of a preposition. The examples below plus the ones in *Write Source 2000* (442.6 - 443.1) illustrate these two uses.

EXAMPLES

I **called Carla about our history assignment.**
(*I* is a subject pronoun.)

"This is *she,"* Carla said when answering the phone.
(*She* is also a subject pronoun used after a *be* verb.)

There are many similarities between *you* and *me.*
(*You* and *me* are object pronouns.)

Directions In each of the following sentences, circle the correct pronoun in parentheses. Write *subject* on the line if the pronoun is a subject pronoun. Write *object* on the line if the pronoun is an object pronoun. The first one has been done for you.

subject **1.** Carla and (*I,* me) love to talk on the phone.

_____ **2.** The telephone is the most wonderful part of technology for

(we, us).

_____ **3.** When someone asks for you on the telephone, do you say,

_____ "This is (she, her)" or "This is (he, him)"?

_____ **4.** (We, Us) both learned quickly how to recognize each other's

voice on the phone.

_____ **5.** On account of (I, me), my mom rarely uses the phone.

All Write p. 381

_____ **6.** *(She, Her)* said the phone company should bill *(I, me)* every

_____ month.

_____ **7.** If my parents were interested, there are so many ways for

(they, them) to improve our telephone setup.

_____ **8.** Without you and *(I, me)*, our families would be so boring.

_____ **9.** Should you and *(I, me)* go swimming this weekend?

_____ **10.** Please let *(I, me)* know about your grandmother.

_____ **11.** Mr. Smith is okay; *(he, him)* lets everyone talk at the end of

class.

_____ **12.** Tomorrow's lunch is Katie's favorite; *(she, her)* just loves

spaghetti casserole.

_____ **13.** The school cooks work hard; *(they, them)* just can't cook like

my mom.

_____ **14.** Who is going to the dance with *(they, them)*?

_____ **15.** Don't believe what Josie said about Linda and *(I, me)*; I never

_____ said that I didn't like *(she, her)*.

Next Step Re-create part of a typical phone conversation with a friend.
Circle two subject pronouns and two object pronouns in your writing.
Share your results.

Possessive Pronouns

Possessive pronouns make your writing read more smoothly. Instead of repeating the same noun or pronoun, you can use the appropriate possessive pronouns, as in the examples below. (See 443.2 in *Write Source 2000* for more information.)

EXAMPLES

Sheila wanted to use (Sheila's) cellular phone.
(Sounds stilted.)

Sheila wanted to use her cellular phone.
(Sounds much better.)

Sheila and I both needed to call (Sheila's and my) parents.
(Needs a possessive pronoun to stand for "Sheila and I.")

She and I both needed to call our parents.
(Correct)

Directions On the blank before each sentence, write the correct possessive pronoun to replace the nouns or pronouns in parentheses. The first one has been done for you.

1. ___*his*___ Alexander Graham Bell tested *(Alexander Graham Bell's)* famous invention for the first time on March 10, 1876.

2. _____ Bell and Thomas Watson had *(Bell and Watson's)* first telephone communication after an accident involving Bell.

3. _____ The telephone is handy for all kinds of emergencies, and *(the telephone's)* first use was a sort of 911 call.

4. _____ Bell had just spilled battery acid on *(Bell's)* pants and called Watson on the telephone in the next room for help.

5. _____ Imagine what you might have said if you had just spilled acid on *(you)* clothes!

All Write p. 381

6. _____ "Watson, come here! I need you!" Bell said urgently into *(Bell's)* newfangled, untested device.

7. _____ We have to use *(we)* imaginations to envision what happened next.

8. _____ In the days and months that followed, Amos E. Dolbear, Elisha Gray, and other inventors claimed that *(Dolbear's, Gray's, and others')* telephone inventions had preceded Bell's.

9. _____ Over 600 claims were made against Alexander Graham Bell before *(Bell's)* claim of having been the first to invent the telephone was upheld by the U.S. Supreme Court.

10. _____ I appreciate hearing this story about Alexander Graham Bell, but one of *(I)* little questions has not been answered.

11. _____ Why did the Bell Telephone Company nickname itself "Ma Bell" if *(Bell Telephone Company's)* founder was actually "Pa" Bell?

12. _____ No matter which company provides it, people want *(people's)* telephone service to be fast, clear, and reasonably priced.

Next Step Create the dialogue that might have occurred between Bell and Watson after Bell's initial call for help. Underline the possessive pronouns you use. If necessary, refer to your handbook for help with punctuating dialogue.

Indefinite Pronouns

Indefinite pronouns do not have a specific antecedent. Some examples of indefinite pronouns are *any, either, none,* and *several.* Turn to 445.2 in *Write Source 2000* for a complete list.

Be certain that these pronouns, when they are used as subjects, agree with their verbs. (Refer to page 89 in *Write Source 2000*.) See the examples below.

EXAMPLES

Singular indefinite pronouns such as *each, either, one,* and *everybody* use a singular verb.

Everybody (wants) **pearly white teeth.**

The indefinite pronouns *all, any, most, none,* and *some* can be either singular or plural. How do you know which is which? Look at the prepositional phrase that follows the indefinite pronoun. If the noun in that phrase is singular, use a singular verb. If the noun is plural, use a plural verb.

Most **of my life** (is) **pretty boring.**
(*Life* is singular so the subject, *most,* takes a singular verb.)

Most **of my dental appointments, however,** (are) **not boring enough.**
(*Appointments* is plural, so the subject, *most,* takes a plural verb.)

Directions In the following sentences, underline the indefinite pronoun subjects once. Circle the correct verb in parentheses. The first one has been done for you.

1. Everyone *(know,* (knows)*)* you're supposed to visit a dentist twice a year.

2. Nobody *(put, puts)* this in the same category as a visit to Disneyland.

3. Most of the dental offices nowadays *(are, is)* set up to calm the fears

   of nervous patients.

4. Nothing *(bother, bothers)* me too much about going to the dentist,

   except one thing.

All Write pp. 52 and 382

5. Sooner or later, somebody in the office *(get, gets)* around to the crucial question.

6. One of the hygienists *(ask, asks)* cheerfully, "So, how's the flossing going?"

7. First of all, almost all of the dentist's hand *(are, is)* usually in my mouth at this moment.

8. No one *(want, wants)* to talk at a time like this.

9. And none of the kids I know *(confess, confesses)* that they usually forget to floss.

10. The truth is that only some of my teeth *(are, is)* easy to slip floss between.

11. *(Do, Does)* anyone have a perfect flossing record?

12. I'm always happy when someone *(hand, hands)* me my new toothbrush, and I can leave.

Next Step What's the best thing about visiting the dentist? What's your least favorite part? Write a paragraph that answers these questions. Use at least two indefinite pronouns and underline them when you are through.

Verbs 1

Both action and linking verbs are needed in writing. Action verbs add power and punch to a sentence. *Tumble, scream,* and *dream* are examples of action verbs. Linking verbs connect a subject to a noun or an adjective in the predicate. *Is* and *seem* are examples of linking verbs. Look at the example sentences below to see how each kind of verb works. (Turn to 446.1-446.2 in *Write Source 2000* for more examples of action and linking verbs.)

EXAMPLES

Many small children *dream* of becoming firefighters.
(The action verb *dream* tells what children do.)

Actually, fighting fires *is* a difficult, dangerous job.
(The linking verb *is* connects—or links—the subject *fighting* to *job.*)

Directions — Underline the verbs with two lines in the following sentences. Label each verb with an *A* for action or an *L* for linking. (Two of the sentences have compound verbs.) The first sentence has been done for you.

1. Nearly everyone <u><u>knows</u></u> about the great Chicago fire of 1871.
   A

2. On the same night, an even more terrible fire roared through Peshtigo, Wisconsin, 250 miles north.

3. At the time, Peshtigo seemed safe, like any other busy logging town.

4. The summer and fall of 1871 were unusually hot and dry throughout the area.

5. During the night of October 8, numerous small fires started in the dry forests around Peshtigo.

6. Fire brigades worked as hard and as fast as possible.

7. But suddenly the situation grew far worse.

All Write p. 383

8. The sound of an enormous, raging forest fire reached the ears of the terrified residents of Peshtigo.

9. In the darkness and confusion, people panicked and ran in all directions.

10. Two different groups of people dashed toward the river from two directions and met on a small bridge.

11. The people felt confused and frightened.

12. The bridge collapsed.

13. Meanwhile, throughout the area, buildings exploded in the extreme heat.

14. Only people in the river survived.

15. Fifteen hundred lives were lost.

16. Three years later, the determined survivors rebuilt Peshtigo on its previous site.

17. The once forested landscape looks different now.

18. Today, dairy farms cover the countryside.

Next Step Write five sentences about fire prevention and safety in your home. Underline and label the verbs you use, *L* for *linking* and *A* for *action*. If you end up with all linking verbs, write at least two more sentences, this time using action verbs.

Verbs 2

Swing, shimmy, and *shuffle* are lively, active words. They are fun to say and fun to use in your writing. These lively words have one important thing in common: they can all be used as **action verbs.** Not all verbs are action packed. Words like *is, are, was,* and *were* are called **linking verbs** because they "link" subjects to nouns or adjectives. Notice how these verbs work in the following examples. (Turn to 446.1-446.2 in *Write Source 2000* for more about these verbs.)

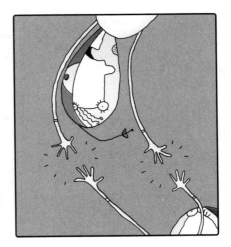

EXAMPLES

Joe expertly *swung* Debbie into the air at the last dance.
(The action verb *swung* describes what Joe did, and it brings the sentence to life.)

Joe and Debbie *are* good dancers.
(*Are* is a linking verb that links the subject *Joe and Debbie* to *dancers.*)

Directions Underline the verb with two lines in each of the following sentences. Label each action verb with an *A* and each linking verb with an *L.* The first two have been done for you.

1. The students *A* <u>entered</u> the dance through the gym door.

2. The decorations *L* <u>were</u> colorful streamers of crepe paper.

3. Our dance began right after school.

4. The theme of our dance was "Friends Forever."

5. Most of the students attended the dance.

6. Our disc jockey played a lot of oldies.

7. Most of us were very nervous at the beginning of the dance.

8. One of the chaperons arranged us in pairs to dance.

9. Larry and Jack hid from the "matchmaker."

10. Robert was the only nondancer in the group.

All Write p. 383

| **Directions** | In the sentences below, underline each verb with two lines. Label each action verb with an *A* and each linking verb with an *L*. The first sentence has been done for you. *Note:* Many of the sentences below are either compound or complex sentences, which means they contain more than one verb. See the examples below as well as the ones in your handbook. |

EXAMPLES

         L   *A*

Because the gym <u>was</u> so hot, we <u>drank</u> a lot of soda.

(A complex sentence contains two clauses.)

   A   *A*

We <u>had</u> fun, though, and the disc jockey <u>told</u> great jokes!

(A compound sentence contains two clauses.)

                   A

1. After the dance, we <u>walked</u> toward the beach.

2. We were hungry, so we stopped at a restaurant.

3. One of our teachers was there, and she asked us about the dance.

4. Larry told her that he was the best dancer there.

5. We all laughed, because Larry is a terrible dancer.

6. Down at the beach, the surf sounded louder than usual.

7. According to Debbie, the TV news predicted a storm.

8. Rick said that the storm was Larry's fault.

9. "Your lousy dancing started a storm, Larry!"

10. Everyone laughed at the joke, including Larry.

Next Step Write three sentences about your own dancing experiences. (If you've never been to a dance, how about a birthday party with dancing?) Underline and label (*A* or *L*) the verbs in your sentences. Share your results.

Helping Verbs

Auxiliary or **helping verbs** come before the main verbs; they help qualify main verbs—telling more exactly when and how the action of a sentence is taking place. Forms of *be, has,* and *do* are commonly used as helping verbs. (Turn to 446.3 in *Write Source 2000* for more information and a list of helping verbs.)

EXAMPLES

The dance <u>was enjoyed</u> by almost everyone.

(*Was* is the helping verb; *enjoyed* is the main verb.)

The organizers <u>could have sold</u> at least 50 more tickets.

(*Could* and *have* are helping verbs; *sold* is the main verb.)

Directions In each of the following sentences, underline the verb with two lines. All but two sentences contain auxiliary or helping verbs.

1. However, the gymnasium at Fillmorton Recreation Center had become a disaster area.

2. Three students had been selected as the cleanup committee.

3. They were moving slowly through the debris on the gym floor.

4. They found Moe Epstein's baseball cap.

5. He may have lost it during his dance with Sasha Seabury.

6. Earlier, they had discovered Rachel Sveum's retainer under a heap of crepe-paper streamers.

7. She probably lost it during the swing contest.

8. That may have been the highlight of the dance.

Next Step Write three sentences on a subject of your choice. Use a form of the auxiliary verb "be" in one of your sentences and a form of the auxiliary verb "has" in another sentence.

All Write p. 383

| **Directions** | In the sentences below, underline each helping verb and circle each main verb. The first sentence has been done for you. |

1. Everyone should (stay) and (help) with the cleanup.

2. But Rick reminded us that a storm was coming and we had planned to walk home.

3. Larry said he could call his dad.

4. "Maybe he can drive us home."

5. Larry called home, but no one answered.

6. Just then, we heard thunder.

7. A blast of wind cut through the gym and blew trash everywhere.

8. "Okay, I am not walking home in a storm," Debbie said.

9. We were wondering what to do when Larry yelled, "Dad!"

10. We all looked up and saw Larry's dad in the car right outside the gym door.

Next Step Write two or three sentences of conversation between Larry's dad and Larry and his friends on the way home. Use quotation marks correctly; underline the helping verbs and circle all main verbs.

Verb Tenses 1

We depend on a watch or clock for the time—except when we are reading or writing, that is. Then we must depend on the **tenses** of verbs to help us keep track of time. Verbs don't tell us if it's 1:30 in the morning or 3:05 in the afternoon. That's clock time. Verbs refer to time in a different way.

The **simple tenses** of verbs indicate whether an action takes place in the present, past, or future. The **perfect tenses** of verbs indicate special segments of time—such as when an action beginning in the past continues into the present. (Turn to 448.1-448.6 in *Write Source 2000* for more information and examples.)

| **Directions** | For each of the verbs that follow, write sentences expressing the tenses, or "times," asked for. The first one has been done for you. |

throw

_____
I always throw potato peelings to the ducks.
(present)

_____
I threw potato peelings to the ducks.
(past)

_____
I have thrown potato peelings to the ducks.
(present perfect)

bring

_____
(past)

_____
(future)

_____
(past perfect)

All Write p. 385

write

_____

(present)

_____

(past)

_____

(past perfect)

take

_____

(present)

_____

(future)

_____

(present perfect)

Next Step Create another tense-writing frame for a verb of your own choosing in the space provided below. Exchange your work with a classmate and complete each other's frame.

_____

(a verb of your choice)

_____

(tense of your choice)

_____

(tense of your choice)

_____

(tense of your choice)

Verb Tenses 2

There are three simple tenses and three perfect tenses. By knowing how to use all six you will be able to tell exactly when the action of your sentences is taking place. (Turn to 448.1-448.6 in *Write Source 2000* for more detailed explanations and examples of verb tenses.)

EXAMPLES

Present Tense:
I *eat.*

Present Perfect:
I *have eaten.*

Past Tense:
I *ate.*

Past Perfect:
I *had eaten.*

Future Tense:
I *will eat.*

Future Perfect:
I *will have eaten.*

Directions   Create sentences for each of the irregular verbs below. (See page 449 in *Write Source 2000* for a chart of these verbs.) Use the pronoun subject (*I, he, you,* etc.) and the tense, or "time," asked for. The first one has been done for you.

1. sing *(we + future tense)*

   We will sing in the choir on Sunday.
   _____

2. lie (recline) *(I + past tense)*

   _____

3. eat *(they + past perfect tense)*

   _____

4. dive *(she + past tense)*

   _____

All Write pp. 385-389

5. break *(I + present perfect tense)*

_____

6. go *(we + future perfect tense)*

_____

7. freeze *(I + past perfect tense)*

_____

8. ride *(she + future tense)*

_____

9. drink *(he + present perfect tense)*

_____

10. steal *(they + past tense)*

_____

Next Step Write a simple story based on your sentence number 10 above. Then rewrite your past tense story using one of the "perfect" tenses. Compare your results.

Irregular Verbs 1

The principal parts of most verbs are formed by adding "ed" to the main verb *(squish, squished, squished).* The principal parts of irregular verbs follow no set pattern *(bite, bit, bitten).*

Let's suppose you've been hired as an editor or a proofreader for your favorite magazine. You start reading through the stack of copy that's piled on your desk. Suddenly, you break out in a cold sweat. Every sentence seems to contain an **irregular verb.** Remembering the different forms of verbs like *burst, bring,* and *shake* drives you crazy.

What are you going to do?

Here's a suggestion: Turn to page 449 in *Write Source 2000* for a chart of irregular verbs. It will answer your questions about these troublesome words . . . and help you keep your job. You will also benefit from the following practice that addresses many of the words listed in the chart.

| Directions | Study these irregular verbs. Read them quietly to yourself several times. |

Present Tense	Past Tense	Past Participle
break	broke	broken
drive	drove	driven
eat	ate	eaten
fall	fell	fallen
give	gave	given
ride	rode	ridden

Note that these verbs have a certain rhythm that helps them stick in your mind. Now try some more.

Present Tense	Past Tense	Past Participle
catch	caught	caught
fly	flew	flown
rise	rose	risen
teach	taught	taught
wear	wore	worn
write	wrote	written

All Write pp. 388-389

Directions After carefully studying the chart of irregular verbs in your handbook, fill in the blank spaces below. (Have your handbook closed as you do your work. Refer to it only after completing your work.) Share your results with a classmate.

Present Tense	Past Tense	Past Participle
begin		
bring		brought
	burst	
do		
	drew	
		frozen
go		
grow		
		led
	saw	
shake	shook	
		sung
steal		
	took	
throw		
		woven

Next Step Write five sentences in which you purposely misuse some of the irregular verbs covered in this activity. (On the back of your paper, write each sentence correctly.) Submit your work for a class pool of "irregular" sentences that can be used for additional review work.

Irregular Verbs 2

Regular verbs follow a simple pattern. You simply add *-ed* to make the past tense and the past participle. Irregular verbs do not follow a simple pattern. Often, you use completely different spellings to make the past forms. Organizing irregular verbs into groups will help you remember them. (Turn to the chart on page 449 in *Write Source 2000*.)

| **Directions** | Using the chart of irregular verbs in your handbook, find the verbs that fit into each of the patterns below. After you complete your lists, read them over to yourself every now and then. Soon you will know these irregular verbs by heart. |

1. Look for the eight verbs that change only one vowel from present tense to past tense to the past participle. Write the three forms of each.

   begin   began   begun _____

   _____   _____

   _____   _____

   _____   _____

2. Write two verbs whose principal parts (present tense, past tense, and past participle) are exactly the same.

   _____   _____

3. Find two verbs that have the same present-tense and past-participle forms. Only the past tense is different. Write the three forms of each.

   _____   _____

All Write pp. 388-389

4. A number of verbs in the handbook chart use the same form for the past and the past participle. Find eight of these verbs and write the three forms of each.

bring   brought   brought

_____   _____

_____   _____

_____   _____

5. Most of the remaining irregular verbs spell each of their three forms differently, with the past participle ending in an _n_ or an _en_. List the three forms for 10 of this type. (There are many more!)

bite   bit   bitten

_____   _____

_____   _____

_____   _____

6. Finally, there are three verbs that don't fit any of the patterns you've just learned. Because they are used often, learn these, too.

_____   _____

_____

Next Step Read through your lists of irregular verbs. Read them again . . . and again. With a partner, quiz each other on the irregular verbs you have learned.

Irregular Verbs Review

| **Directions** | Read each of the sentences below and decide which verb in parentheses is the correct choice. Write your choice on the blank in front of each sentence. The first one has been done for you. *Remember:* When helping verbs like *has, have,* or *had* are used, the past participle is required. (Turn to 449.) |

_____*seen*_____ **1.** Have you ever *(seen, saw)* Kansas City?

_____ **2.** I have *(flew, flown)* over the city a couple of times, but I have never actually visited it.

_____ **3.** Kansas City *(growed, grew)* up near the spot where the Missouri and Kansas Rivers meet.

_____ **4.** The possibility for river travel has often *(bringed, brought)* settlers to a place.

_____ **5.** Some early settlers were *(drew, drawn)* to the area because of the trading and business opportunities.

_____ **6.** That's how Kansas City *(came, come)* into existence.

_____ **7.** Four years later, the total population of the city had *(rose, risen)* to only a couple dozen people.

_____ **8.** The town of Independence, 14 miles east of Kansas City, had *(stolen, stole)* all the attention in the area.

_____ **9.** Independence had *(grew, grown)* into a booming frontier city of 3,000 people.

_____ **10.** In Independence, pioneers outfitted their wagons and *(drove, drived)* west along the Santa Fe and Oregon Trails.

_____ **11.** Several events in the 1840's *(gaved, gave)* Kansas City the edge over Independence.

_____ **12.** The Missouri River shifted its course and *(ran, runned)* in a direction favorable to Kansas City.

_____ **13.** The California gold rush *(brought, brang)* 40,000 people through the city.

All Write pp. 388-389

_____ **14.** The town of Independence *(shrinked, shrank)*, but Kansas City grew into twin cities, one in Missouri and one in the Kansas territory.

_____ **15.** Before the Civil War, slaves from Missouri *(come, came)* to Kansas, a free territory.

_____ **16.** Bloody battles were *(fighted, fought)* during the Civil War in Kansas City.

_____ **17.** Today, Kansas City is *(known, knowed)*, among other things, for its cool jazz and great barbeque.

_____ **18.** If you haven't *(ate, eaten)* Kansas City barbeque, you haven't tasted real barbeque, according to the natives.

_____ **19.** Jazz is played and *(sung, sang)* at many clubs across the city.

Next Step Kansas City calls itself the "Heart of the Heartland." Find Kansas City on the map of the United States in your handbook. Approximately how many miles is Kansas City from each of the four U.S. borders? Write a paragraph about what you think of Kansas City's heartland claim. Try to use two or three irregular verbs in your writing.

Transitive and Linking Verbs

Transitive verbs "transfer" their action to a direct object. The direct object completes the meaning of the sentence, as in the examples that follow. Linking verbs do not express action. **Linking verbs** link the subject of a sentence to a noun or an adjective, called the predicate noun or the predicate adjective. (For more information, see 446.2 and 450.1 in *Write Source 2000*.)

EXAMPLES

Transitive Verbs:

I *raise* ducks. I *feed* them.
(*Raise* and *feed* are transitive verbs. Their action is transferred to *ducks* and *them*, the direct objects. Direct objects are always nouns or pronouns.)

Linking Verbs:

Platypuses *are* swimmers.
(*Are* is a linking verb that links the subject, *platypuses*, to the predicate noun, *swimmers*.)

The creature *seemed* frightened.
(*Seemed* is a linking verb that links the subject, *creature*, to the predicate adjective, *frightened*.)

Directions

In the following sentences, underline each verb twice. Circle each direct object, predicate noun, or predicate adjective. (Don't forget that these can be compound. There may be two or three of them!) On the blank write *DO* for direct object, *PN* for predicate noun, or *PA* for predicate adjective. The first sentence has been done for you.

PN   **1.** The platypus is a (native) of Australia and Tasmania.

_____   **2.** Is a platypus a mammal or a bird?

_____   **3.** Scientists argued this matter for years.

_____   **4.** Like birds, platypuses lay eggs.

_____   **5.** Like mammals, platypuses nurse their young.

   All Write pp. 383 and 390-391

_____ **6.** The platypus's feet appear webbed, like an aquatic bird's.

_____ **7.** But their bodies feel soft and furry.

_____ **8.** The duck-billed platypus uses its large, flat bill like a probe.

_____ **9.** Platypuses eat insects, worms, and shellfish.

_____ **10.** To observers, this unusual-looking creature seems shy and sensitive.

_____ **11.** Platypuses are monotremes.

_____ **12.** A monotreme is an egg-laying mammal.

_____ **13.** Platypuses dig long burrows into the banks of ponds or streams.

_____ **14.** At the end of these burrows, platypuses make grass-lined chambers.

_____ **15.** Platypuses are safe in these chambers during the day.

Next Step Describe an animal that you know about by answering these questions: What does the animal look like? Where is it found? What does it eat? Who are its natural enemies? What special abilities does it have? Write a paragraph containing the details you've gathered. Now go back and underline all your main verbs. Circle and label the direct objects, predicate nouns, and predicate adjectives in your sentences.

Subject-Verb Agreement 1

Here are some definite signs of agreement: a nod of the head, a handshake, and a signature on a contract. Do you know of any others? Here's one that has to do with writing and speaking. A singular subject *(my friend)* used with a singular verb *(listens)* is a definite sign of agreement. In the same way, a plural subject *(my friends)* used with a plural verb *(listen)* is another sign of agreement.

Subjects and verbs used together must agree in number. That is, they must both be singular or plural. Study the examples below to see what we mean. (Also turn to pages 88-89 in *Write Source 2000* for more information.)

EXAMPLES

My <u>friends</u> <u><u>go</u></u> with me every year to the state fair.

(Both the subject and verb are plural, so they agree.)

<u>Carlos</u> and <u>I</u> <u><u>ride</u></u> the rocket cars.

(Compound subjects connected by *and* require plural verbs. *Ride* is plural.)

<u>Everyone</u> <u><u>enjoys</u></u> the music in the grandstand area.

(Indefinite pronouns like *everyone* require singular verbs. *Enjoys* is a singular verb, so the subject and verb agree.)

Neither <u>Alfredo</u> nor <u>Jim</u> <u><u>likes</u></u> amusement rides.

(With compound subjects connected by *or* or *nor*, the verb must agree with the subject nearest the verb. *Jim* is singular, so *likes* is singular.)

Directions In each sentence, the subject is underlined with one line and the verb with two lines. Put a check next to each sentence in which the subject and verb do not agree. For those sentences you check, correct the subject-verb agreement errors. The first sentence has been done for you.

is

✔_____ **1.** At the fair, the <u>parade</u> of draft horses ~~<u><u>are</u></u>~~ going to be on Sunday.

_____ **2.** <u>One</u> of my friends <u><u>goes</u></u> immediately to see the sideshows.

All Write pp. 51-52

_____ **3.** Cotton candy and caramel corn is my favorite snacks.

_____ **4.** Carlos and I saves our money for the rides.

_____ **5.** Jeremy and Zach tries to win goldfish and stuffed animals.

_____ **6.** The double Ferris wheel or the parachute drop is my favorite ride.

_____ **7.** John, as well as my other friends, love the bumper cars.

_____ **8.** My sister and Mary always go on the Tilt-A-Whirl ride.

_____ **9.** A water ride or a roller coaster are the coolest ride on a hot day.

_____ **10.** Neither Julie nor Sally visit the animal barns.

_____ **11.** Everybody likes to watch the pig races.

_____ **12.** The pigs run much faster than you would think.

_____ **13.** One of the pigs run professionally.

_____ **14.** We all loves the fair more than any other summertime activity.

Next Step Use your own paper to write about a time when you *disagreed* with a friend, a brother or sister, a teacher, or someone else about something.   Don't forget that subjects and verbs must agree in all types of writing—even when you are writing about "disagreeable" topics. Share your results.

Subject-Verb Agreement 2

In order to check for subject-verb agreement, you must first identify the main subject and its verb. Underlining the main subject once and the verb twice in your rough drafts will help you look for subject-verb agreement in your own writing. (Turn to pages 88-89 in *Write Source 2000* for help with special kinds of agreement problems.)

| **Directions** | Proofread the following passage. Underline the main subjects once and the verbs twice. Then check for subject-verb agreement problems. When you find an error, cross it out and write the correct word above it. The first sentence has been done for you. (If a sentence is correct, don't change it.) |

1   A <u>triathlon</u>, with its combination of swimming, bicycling, and running,

        is

2   ~~are~~ one of the most grueling sports events ever. The Ironman Triathlon, in

3   Oahu, Hawaii, have become the ultimate sports challenge among super

4   athletes from all over the world. Of course, Hawaii's picture-perfect scenery

5   and ideal climate probably doesn't hurt attendance any. A triathlon consists

6   of the following events. First, each competitor swims 2.4 miles in the sea.

7   After that, they all bikes for 112 miles. To top it off, all competitors runs a

8   28-mile marathon. Yes, most of the competitors actually cross the finish

9   line.

    All Write pp. 51-52

10   My two aunts, Helga and Sue, has been training for a minitriathlon.

11   Shorter distances makes a minitriathlon more tolerable for an average,

12   well-trained athlete. Neither of my aunts has competed in a triathlon

13   before this year. Some in my family calls Helga and Sue crazy. Those

14   people probably feels jealous of my aunts. I, as well as most of my friends,

15   admire my aunts' determination. Each of them are doing the triathlon for

16   personal reasons. In my book, they is very cool.

Next Step Use the "American to Metric Table" in your handbook to convert the distances for the three triathlon events into meters.

Subject-Verb Agreement Review

Turn to pages 88-89 in *Write Source 2000* to review the explanations and examples of some tricky subject-verb agreement problems.

| **Directions** | On the blank at the beginning of each sentence, write the correct verb choice from the pair in parentheses. The first one has been done for you. |

1. ___*has*___ Someone just like you *(has, have)* invented every human-made object in the world.

2. _____ One of the tastiest inventions *(was, were)* created by accident.

3. _____ Imagine this scene. A certain Lord Montagu and his friends *(is, are)* enjoying a friendly game of cards 200 years ago in merry old England.

4. _____ In the middle of a particularly intense round of cards, nobody *(want, wants)* to stop for lunch.

5. _____ Either Lord Montagu or his friends *(ring, rings)* for a servant to bring food to the table.

6. _____ The servant, in a well-ironed, black-and-white uniform, *(bring, brings)* in a tray of bread and meat.

7. _____ On the table *(lay, lays)* the cards, one piled on top of the other.

All Write pp. 51-52

8. _____ Suddenly, into Lord Montagu's head, *(pop, pops)* the bright idea of stacking the bread and meat in a similar way.

9. _____ Everyone around the table *(is, are)* delighted.

10. _____ Most of the group *(find, finds)* they can eat and play cards at the same time.

11. _____ News of the exciting invention *(travel, travels)* quickly.

12. _____ The whole concoction *(become, becomes)* known as a *sandwich* in honor of Lord Montagu, the fourth earl of Sandwich.

Next Step New inventions come from people who are looking for a better (faster, easier, cheaper) way of doing something. Create a new product or modify an old product with new ideas. Describe your invention in a few short sentences and share your writing with your classmates.

Adjectives

Your best writing starts with a good writing topic. You must have a good story to tell (or some interesting facts to present). Then you must tell your story well. Specific nouns and action-packed verbs can add a great deal to your writing. **Adjectives,** which modify nouns or pronouns, can also help you tell a good story. Study the examples below to see how adjectives work. (Also turn to page 136 and then 451.4-452.5 in *Write Source 2000* for more information and examples.)

EXAMPLES

Steve participated in two school activities.
(The adjective *two* describes how many activities. The adjective *school* describes what kind of activities.)

Yesterday, Steve left his baseball on the bus.
(The possessive pronoun *his* describes which baseball.)

Directions	Underline the adjectives in the following sentences. The articles *a, an,* and *the* should not be considered adjectives in this activity. (The number of adjectives in each sentence is indicated in parentheses.) The first one has been done for you.

1. Steve played on the sixth-grade soccer team. (2)

2. He also played first cornet in the jazz band. (2)

3. Steve was excited about the upcoming weekend. (2)

4. On Friday night, his parents were going to let him pitch their umbrella tent in the backyard. (4)

5. He had invited Dave and Greg and three other friends from his crowd. (3)

6. That night, they ran an extension cord from the nearby house and watched movies on a VCR until midnight. (3)

All Write pp. 93 and 393-395

7. Dave said, "Shelly and some of her friends are sleeping in a small Winnebago camper at her house." (4)

8. At 12:30, the six guys sneaked over there and rocked the camper. (1)

9. The aluminum camper was dark and empty, so they went home. (3)

10. A note taped to one of the tent flaps said, "Sorry we missed you at the camper. See you first hour on Monday." (2)

11. Later, Greg blew some noisemakers from behind a nearby bush. (2)

12. Luckily for Steve, none of his family members or next-door neighbors woke up. (3)

13. For almost a week, Steve felt good about the weekend. (1)

14. Then, Dave wore a screaming Hawaiian shirt to school, and suddenly the camping experience was forgotten. (3)

Next Step Write an acrostic poem like the one below. To write an acrostic poem, use the letters of a word to begin each new line. Each line should say something about the word. Have the poem describe an idea or a feeling like *love, freedom,* or *shyness.*

Example:

    Lifting my heart
    Over my head is
    Very hard to do,
    Except when you're around.

Note: An acrostic poem is also called a "title-down" poem.

Special Kinds of Adjectives

All adjectives describe nouns or pronouns. A predicate adjective is an adjective that follows a linking verb and describes the subject of a sentence, as in the examples below. (For more information on how linking verbs and predicate adjectives work together, see 446.2 and 452.5 in *Write Source 2000*.)

EXAMPLES

Bats feel *soft* to the touch.
(*Soft* is a predicate adjective linked to the subject *bats* by the verb *feel*.)

Bats are *fascinating*.
(*Fascinating* is a predicate adjective linked to the subject *bats* by the verb *are*.)

Directions — Underline each subject once and each linking verb twice in the following sentences. Circle each predicate adjective. The first two sentences have been done for you.

1. Do bats seem (frightening) or (mysterious) to you?

2. It is (true) that bats are (scary) to many people.

3. Perhaps bats are mysterious and frightening because of their lifestyle.

4. Most bats remain hidden in dark caves during the day.

5. Bats are nocturnal, which means they are active at night.

6. A bat's webbed wings and big ears look unusual to some people.

7. Many people remain afraid of bats out of ignorance.

8. A healthy respect is good because bats can be rabid.

9. But bats are valuable, too, for preying on mice, mosquitoes, and other pests.

All Write pp. 383 and 394

10. Through widespread slaughter and environmental damage, some bat species became rare in the 1980's.

11. Scientists appear concerned that the disappearance of bats could be upsetting to the earth's ecology.

12. For one thing, bats are valuable because they pollinate plants as they feed.

13. Bats are also useful for spreading the seeds of fruits, trees, and flowers.

14. It is popular to care about whales, wolves, and spotted owls; but bats are worthy, too.

Next Step To find out more about bats and how you can help keep them off the endangered list, write a letter to Bat Conservation International, P.O. Box 162603, Austin, TX 78716.

Forms of Adjectives

The *positive* form of an adjective does not compare a noun to anything else (*tall* building). The *comparative* form compares two nouns (*taller* building). The *superlative* form compares three or more nouns (*tallest* building). Some adjectives have irregular forms (*good, better, best* and *bad, worse, worst*). Others add *more* in the comparative form and *most* in the superlative form. (For more information, see 453.1-453.6 in *Write Source 2000*.)

EXAMPLES

Positive Forms:
California is a *big* state.
New York is a *populous* state.

Comparative Forms:
Texas is *bigger* than California.
Texas is *more populous* than Alaska.

Superlative Forms:
Alaska is the *biggest* state of all.
California is the *most populous* state of all.

Directions In the following sentences, underline the correct form of the adjective in the parentheses. In the blank in front of each sentence, write *P* for positive, *C* for comparative, or *S* for superlative to indicate which form it is. The first sentence has been done for you.

1. ____*S*____ What is the (*gigantic, most gigantic*) country in the world?

2. _____ Out of all of the countries, Russia is by far the (*more massive,*

   most massive) with more than 6.5 million square miles within

   its borders.

3. _____ Canada is slightly (*larger, more larger*) than the United States

   _____ in size, but its population is much (*smaller, more smaller*).

All Write p. 395

4. _____ China, of course, has the *(greatest, most greatest)* number of

people—1.2 billion—of all the countries in the world.

5. _____ According to the United Nations, India's population was four

times *(bigger, more bigger)* than the United States's population

in 1997.

6. _____ By the year 2050, the United Nations predicts that India will

have grown *(larger, more larger)* than China in population.

7. _____ In that same year, the five *(more, most)* populous countries in the

world will be (1) India, (2) China, (3) Pakistan, (4) the United

States, and (5) Nigeria.

8. _____ Did you notice that the three *(bigger, biggest)* countries in terms

of population are all in Asia?

9. _____ Vatican City, surrounded by Rome on all sides, is the *(smallest,*

most smallest) country in the world. It is 1/5 of a square mile.

10. _____ Whether you live in a *(large, more large)* country or in a

_____ *(small, more small)* one doesn't matter.

11. _____ You are *(unique, more unique)*; no one is quite like you.

12. _____ According to the great humanitarians, no person is

(importanter, more important) than another.

Next Step Find the "Geographic Facts" page in your "Student Almanac."
Write four sentences that make comparisons. For example: "The
Pacific Ocean is the largest ocean." Then exchange papers with a
classmate and underline the adjectives. Label each other's sentences
with a *P,* an *S,* or a *C* as you did above.

Colorful Adjectives 1

Whenever possible, use colorful adjectives to describe the nouns in your writing. At times, you'll need to dig deep to find just the right word to modify a certain noun. See the example below. (Also turn to page 136 in *Write Source 2000* for more information.)

EXAMPLE

The pencil bird is known for its <u>uncommon</u> eggs.

_____*gigantic*_____   _____*patterned*_____

(The words *gigantic* and *patterned* are more colorful than *uncommon*.)

Directions   Write three colorful adjectives that could be used instead of the overused adjective underlined in each sentence. (If you think you need help, use a thesaurus for this exercise.)

1. Harvey Kennedy had a <u>good</u> idea for an invention—the shoelace. He earned more than $2,000,000 for his idea.

_____   _____   _____

2. Walter Hunt made a <u>bad</u> decision when he sold his safety-pin patent for $400. He never received any more money for his invention.

_____   _____   _____

3. Hyman Lipman had a <u>nice</u> idea when he combined a pencil with an eraser. He sold his patent for $100,000 in 1858.

_____   _____   _____

4. One man earned money in a <u>different</u> way. He allowed an advertising company to completely paint his van with ads.

_____   _____   _____

 Next Step Decide which new adjective works best in each sentence. Circle your answer. Afterward share your work with a classmate.

All Write p. 93

Colorful Adjectives 2

When you choose an adjective to modify a certain noun, make sure it adds color to the noun in question and that it expresses the right feeling. (Turn to page 136 in *Write Source 2000* for more information about the connotation of words.)

Directions | **Fill in each blank in the paragraph with one of the two words listed. Choose the word that expresses the right meaning and feeling. (The two italicized words in the first sentence set the tone for the rest of the paragraph.)**

1   My world is overflowing with *impatient* and *thoughtless* people. Sadly,

2   many of these _____ people seem to be in the local shopping
                          (weird, impolite)

3   malls every time I go there. I can't count how often I've been bumped by

4   _____ shoppers, snapped at by _____ clerks, and
         (rude, nervous)   *(angry, grouchy)*

5   pestered by _____ children running up and down aisles.
                   (complaining, wild)

6   Many people seem to think that shopping is a competition to be won. While

7   a shopping trip used to be an enjoyable, _____ time, lately it's
                                                (relaxing, comforting)

8   more likely to end up being an _____ afternoon full of
                                       (exhausting, sickening)

9   _____ experiences. I'd rather stay home and clean my
     (unpleasant, terrifying)

10   bedroom than make even one more shopping trip. Well, almost.

Types of Adverbs

Words like *loudly, really, very,* and *never* are classified as adverbs. They are used to modify verbs, adjectives, or other adverbs. Adverbs fall into four different types or classes: adverbs of *time, place, manner,* and *degree.* (Turn to 454.2 in *Write Source 2000* for more information.)

EXAMPLE

Yesterday, Laura *hurriedly* flew *over* to inspect the dumpsite and *almost* fainted from the stench.

| Directions | In the chart below, arrange the following list of adverbs according to the four different types. There are five adverbs per category. (Four have already been "charted" for you.) |

yesterday	really	lazily	there	soon
over	carefully	daily	nervously	scarcely
hurriedly	forward	here	very	everywhere
almost	tomorrow	hardly	before	brilliantly

Time (answers *when*)	Place (answers *where*)	Manner (answers *how*)	Degree (answers *to what extent*)
yesterday	*over*	*hurriedly*	*almost*

Next Step As a special challenge, add at least one more adverb to each of the four categories above.

All Write p. 396

Directions Write one sentence using an example of each type of adverb listed below. (Use the adverbs you charted on the previous page in your sentences.)

adverb of time _____

_____

_____

adverb of place _____

_____

_____

adverb of manner _____

_____

_____

adverb of degree _____

_____

_____

Special Challenge: Really lay it on thick by using three or more of the adverbs from the chart in one sentence. (Write your sentence in the space below.)

_____

_____

_____

Next Step Use adverbs in a fun way by creating at least one Tom Swifty. Two examples follow:

"Look at that punctured tire," my dad said flatly.
"Stay down," the sergeant whispered lowly.

In both examples, the underlined adverbs turn the statements into Tom Swifties.

Forms of Adverbs

Adverbs also have positive, comparative, and superlative forms. As with adjectives, some adverbs use *more* or *most* to form comparative and superlative forms. Other adverbs (such as *well, better, best*) are irregular and do not follow the normal pattern. (Refer to 454.1 in *Write Source 2000* for more information.)

EXAMPLES

Positive Forms:
Joel runs *fast*.
Carlos reads *rapidly*.

Comparative Forms:
Joel runs *faster* than Carlos.
Carlos reads *more rapidly* than Joel.

Superlative Forms:
Ernesto runs the *fastest* of all.
Juan reads the *most rapidly* in our class.

Directions   In the following sentences, underline the correct adverb form from the two in parentheses and write *P* for positive, *C* for comparative, or *S* for superlative on the line before each sentence. The first one has been done for you.

1. __*P*__ The first rules for soccer were published in London in 1863; but since then, the popularity of the sport has spread (*rapidly*, *more rapidly*) across the globe.

2. _____ You must have good legs and lots of energy if you want to play soccer (*more well, well*).

3. _____ Soccer is played (*less often, least often*) than basketball in the United States.

All Write p. 397

4. _____ Around the world, 100 million people of all ages and ability levels

play soccer *(enthusiastically, more enthusiastically)*.

5. _____ Over the years, soccer has *(steadily, most steadily)* become more

popular.

6. _____ Soccer's popularity among women is growing *(rapider, more rapidly)*

than field hockey's popularity.

| **Directions** | Fill in an appropriate adverb in each sentence below. |

1. On good days, I can run _____ .

2. In the last game, I played _____ .

3. Of all the sports, I love soccer _____ .

4. I would rather go to practice on Saturday morning than sleep

_____ .

5. I practice _____ than my teammates do.

6. _____ , my team has been losing.

7. I need to work _____ on my kicking.

8. Kicking the ball _____ past the goalie is hard.

Next Step Think of three sports that you enjoy watching or playing. Think of facts you know and your feelings about each sport. Write a paragraph comparing these three sports. Use at least one positive, one comparative, and one superlative form of an adverb in your writing.

Prepositional Phrases

A preposition is like a train engine. It has to pull something before it is useful. A preposition pulls adjectives, adverbs, and noun or pronoun objects. A prepositional train (actually a *prepositional phrase*) is a preposition and all of the related words it pulls.

EXAMPLES

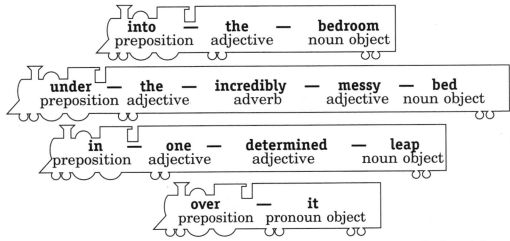

into	**the**	**bedroom**
preposition	adjective	noun object

under	**the**	**incredibly**	**messy**	**bed**
preposition	adjective	adverb	adjective	noun object

in	**one**	**determined**	**leap**
preposition	adjective	adjective	noun object

over	**it**
preposition	pronoun object

Note: The words *a*, *an*, and *the* are special types of adjectives called articles.

Directions | Make three prepositional trains of your own, using the list of prepositions in the handbook as a general guide. (Turn to 455.3 in *Write Source 2000* for this information.)

Next Step As a special challenge, label the parts in your trains as shown in the examples above.

All Write p. 398

Directions   In the space below, use each of your prepositional trains in a sentence.

1. _____

   _____

2. _____

   _____

3. _____

   _____

Directions   On the lines below, keep writing the same sentence, but change the preposition each time—as many times as possible.

Freezer Breezer swam <u>alongside of</u> the whales.

(Some prepositions like *alongside of* consist of two words.)

Freezer Breezer swam <u>under</u> the whales. _____

_____

_____

_____

_____

_____

_____

_____

Next Step Exchange your work with a classmate and see who was able to use the most prepositions.

Interjections

An **interjection** is a word that expresses strong emotion or surprise. Interjections are especially useful when you are writing dialogue for a play or a story. Either an exclamation point or a comma is used to separate an interjection from the rest of the sentence. (Turn to page 453 in *Write Source 2000* for more about interjections.) Note the interjections (underlined) in the following examples.

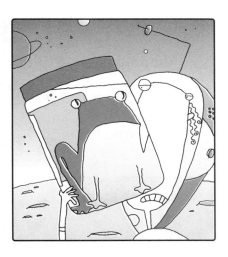

EXAMPLES

Yech! Why do we have to study pickled frogs?

Hmm, I think I'll leave mine in the jar.

Directions Underline each interjection in the story that follows. Supply an interjection when a space is provided. The first one has been done for you.

1   "Wow, Camille! Look at that!" screamed Jana.

2   "Good grief, Jana, what is your problem?"

3   "_____ !" You're not going to believe this, but

4   my pickled frog just moved inside the jar."

5   "Oh, sure, and my frog has wings," laughed Camille.

6   "Hey, I'm telling the truth. Look for yourself if you don't believe me."

7   "Okay, but this better not be a trick. You know how much I like

8   surprises," warned Camille.

9   "No way, this is the real thing. I'll take the lid off the jar so you can

10   get a closer look."

11   "_____ !" screamed Camille as the frog

12   jumped out of the jar, into her lap, and onto the floor.

All Write p. 397

13   "_____ ! Just moving was bad enough;

14   jumping is too freaky," shuddered Jana.

15   "Where'd it go? _____ , we'd better go find

16   it!" warned Camille.

Directions   Continue the conversation on the lines below. Include at least three additional interjections. (Use your own paper if you need more space.)

_____

_____

_____

_____

_____

_____

_____

_____

_____

_____

_____

_____

_____

_____

Next Step Exchange conversations with a classmate. Note how your partner used interjections in his or her work.

Coordinating Conjunctions

Coordinating conjunctions are needed to connect words, phrases, and clauses in sentences. The parts being connected must be equal or of the same type. (For more information, see 456.1 - 456.4 in *Write Source 2000*.)

EXAMPLES

Do you like to *draw* or *paint?*
(The words *draw* and *paint* are connected by the conjunction *or*.)

I *like to draw*, but *painting is difficult for me*.
(The two clauses of the compound sentence are connected by the conjunction *but*.)

Directions   Circle the coordinating conjunction in each of the following sentences. Underline the parts that the conjunction connects. The first two sentences have been done for you.

1. Because artists created lifelike paintings long before there were cameras, we can see many of the <u>people</u>, <u>places</u>, (and) <u>events</u> of the past.

2. Some artists paint realistic <u>portraits of people</u>, <u>still lifes</u>, (and) <u>landscapes</u>.

3. Three famous landscape artists are Jan Vermeer from Holland, Katsushika Hokusai from Japan, and Georgia O'Keeffe from the United States.

4. Art can express a feeling of happiness, joy, sadness, fear, or rage.

5. The oldest paintings in the world are more than 30,000 years old, yet they were unknown to us until recently.

    All Write p. 399

6. We did not know of the paintings' existence, for they were hidden in caves in southwestern France.

7. We do not know the names of the artists who painted these cave walls, but we do know they were fine artists.

8. They made their paints out of colored earth and animal fat or charcoal.

9. Of course, we cannot know this for sure, but the people who lived long ago probably believed the cave paintings had magical powers.

10. There is something magical about art, but it requires hard work to develop artistic skill.

11. Street artists often attract a crowd, for everyone wants to see how the "magic" is done.

Next Step Write three additional sentences about a street artist or musician you've seen or heard. Use at least one coordinating conjunction in each sentence.

Subordinating Conjunctions

A reader must make many connections in a piece of writing, moving from one idea to the next. To make sure that readers are able to follow ideas smoothly and easily, writers often use **subordinating conjunctions.** See the examples below. (Also turn to 456.1-456.4 in *Write Source 2000* for more information about conjunctions.)

EXAMPLES

Shorter Sentences:
Tasha loves creamed asparagus on toast. Her older brother Michael gags at the sight of this meal.

Combined Sentence:
Tasha loves creamed asparagus on toast, <u>although</u> her older brother Michael gags at the sight of this meal.
(The sentences are connected with the subordinating conjunction *although.*)

Shorter Sentences:
My little sister's swimming pool was "bleeding." I applied a big bandage.

Combined Sentence:
<u>Because</u> my little sister's swimming pool was "bleeding," I applied a big bandage.
(The sentences are connected with the subordinating conjunction *because.*)

Directions	Review the list of conjunctions in your handbook. Then practice using conjunctions by combining the following pairs of brief sentences into longer, smoother-reading ones. Try to use a different connecting word in each of your new sentences.

1. Lucille tried on many bathing suits. Not one of them fit her right.

_____

_____

All Write p. 399

2. Father thought he saw a mermaid. Fred got the big net.

_____

_____

_____

3. Finish your homework. You can go to the park.

_____

_____

_____

4. My dog Oscar's belly almost drags on the ground. I can't bear to put him on a diet.

_____

_____

_____

5. Turn left at this corner. You'll end up in a deep pit.

_____

_____

_____

Next Step Trade papers with a classmate and see what conjunctions your partner used in his or her sentences. Then write three sentences using the following **correlative conjunctions:** *either, or; neither, nor;* and *both, and.*

Conjunctions Review

There are many kinds of conjunctions besides *and, but, or, nor, for, so,* and *yet.* All of them help connect the parts of sentences so that the sentences read smoothly and make sense. (Review page 456 in *Write Source 2000* and look at the list of conjunctions at 456.4.)

Directions	Read the following paragraph of short, choppy sentences. Rewrite the paragraph, using conjunctions so that it flows like "silk." You may drop words or change verb tenses if you need to.

1   The Silk Road was a trade route. It connected China to Rome. People

2   began using this route about 100 B.C. Silk from China was carried on it.

3   Gold from Rome was carried on it. Silver from Rome was carried on it.

4   Caravans met on the road. They traded goods. They traded ideas. The

5   Roman Empire fell apart around A.D. 500. The Silk Road wasn't used much

6   after that time. It had lasted 600 years.

_____

_____

_____

_____

_____

_____

_____

Next Step In ancient times, people had the Silk Road. Today, we have the Information Highway. How will people communicate and trade a hundred years from now? Write your predictions in a paragraph. Use conjunctions.

All Write p. 399

Parts of Speech Review 1

Directions   Each "coin" contains a list of words representing one of the eight parts of speech. Identify the part of speech for each list of words on the blank space provided within each coin. Work on this activity with a partner if your teacher allows it. (Turn to page 457.)

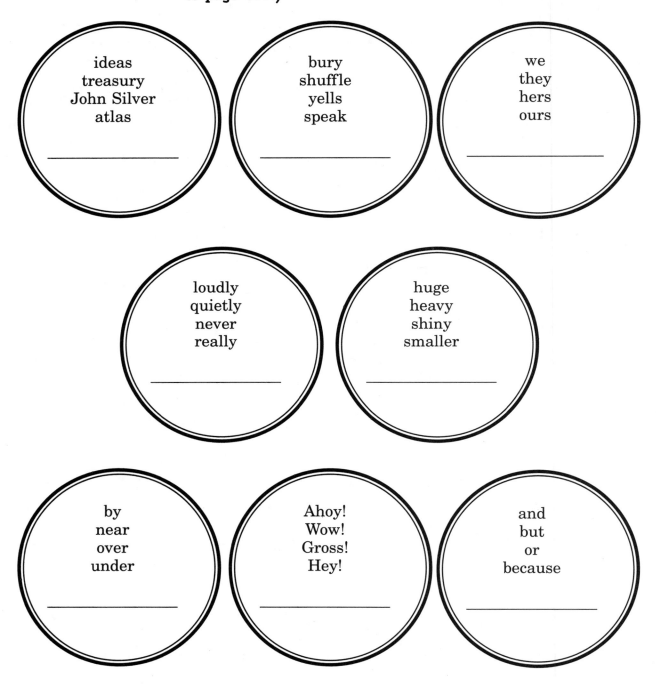

ideas
treasury
John Silver
atlas
_____

bury
shuffle
yells
speak
_____

we
they
hers
ours
_____

loudly
quietly
never
really
_____

huge
heavy
shiny
smaller
_____

by
near
over
under
_____

Ahoy!
Wow!
Gross!
Hey!
_____

and
but
or
because
_____

Parts of Speech Review 2

| **Directions** | Identify the part of speech for each underlined word in the following passage. The first two have been done for you. (Turn to page 457.) |

(Turn to page 457.)

verb   *preposition*

1   Most state names <u>tell</u> you something <u>about</u> the state's beginnings, <u>so</u>

2   it's not <u>surprising</u> that many states have <u>Native American</u> names. After all,

3   <u>who</u> was here first? Chances are fifty-fifty, in fact, that <u>your</u> state name

4   was <u>borrowed</u> from a word in the language <u>of</u> the Native Americans who

5   lived <u>there</u> first. Alabama, Kansas, <u>and</u> Tennessee are three examples of

6   states named after words <u>in</u> the Creek, Sioux, and <u>Cherokee</u> languages.

7   If your state does <u>not</u> have a Native American name, <u>chances</u> are <u>fairly</u>

8   good that it <u>has</u> an English <u>name</u>, especially if it was <u>one</u> of the <u>original</u>

9   colonies. Eight of the <u>thirteen</u> colonies were <u>named</u> after English royalty <u>or</u>

10 places in England. Virginia was named after <u>Queen Elizabeth</u> of England

11 who was <u>called</u> the "Virgin Queen" because she <u>never</u> married. <u>Georgia</u> was

12 named after King George II. (<u>His</u> son was the <u>ruler</u> the colonists <u>fought</u>

13 against <u>during</u> the Revolutionary War.) New Hampshire <u>got</u> its name from

14 a <u>homesick</u> English settler <u>from</u> Hampshire, <u>England</u>, and the same goes <u>for</u>

15 New Jersey, named after the English <u>island</u> of Jersey.

All Write p. 374

16   About half a <u>dozen</u> states, including three of <u>our</u> most <u>heavily</u>

17   populated—Florida, <u>Texas</u>, and California—have <u>Spanish</u> names, while a

18   <u>few</u> have French <u>or</u> Dutch names. That <u>leaves</u> Pennsylvania, which was

19   <u>named</u> after its <u>peace-loving</u> founder, William Penn, and <u>the</u> state of

20   Washington; <u>but</u> I hope you don't <u>need</u> me to tell you who <u>that</u> state was

21   named after. If you don't know, <u>eek!</u> Back to first <u>grade</u> with you!

Next Step Use your classroom or library encyclopedias to learn about the early history of your state. Write a paragraph using the most interesting facts and details you find. Underscore any 10 words and label each according to its part of speech.

Parts of Speech Review 3

| **Directions** | Pair up with a classmate and, as a team, identify the part of speech for each underlined word. There are four examples of each part of speech, except for the interjection, which has two examples. The first two sentences have been done for you. (Turn to page 457.) |

adverb   *preposition*

1   Last Saturday, the public pool <u>finally</u> opened <u>for</u> the summer. My friend

pronoun

2   Sharla and <u>I</u> had been waiting for what seemed like months. Come to think

3   of it, it had been <u>two</u> months. Anyway, we <u>were</u> there bright and early, even

4   though it was only about 65 degrees outside. Sharla was wearing a plain <u>blue</u>

5   <u>bikini</u>. I had <u>eagerly</u> bought a bikini, too, <u>but</u> mine was made from a

6   silvery-green, <u>striped</u> material.

7   Within an hour, the whole neighborhood showed up. <u>Well</u>, there might

8   have been one <u>or</u> two kids missing. Sharla <u>looked</u> like a big, <u>blue-lipped</u>

9   goose bump <u>because</u> the water was so cold. We had a great time, though.

10   Carl and Burton, two boys <u>from</u> the eighth grade, did belly flops off the

11   low-dive until <u>they</u> were covered with red <u>blotches</u>. Sharla and I had an

12   underwater swimming contest, and <u>some</u> of our friends <u>practiced</u>

13   synchronized swimming.

14   There was only one bad moment. As we were walking home, <u>Brad</u>

All Write **p. 374**

15   showed up <u>with</u> a bag of sand, which he started tossing as he yelled, "<u>Hey!</u>"

16   I'm <u>throwing</u> a beach party."

17   <u>We</u> walked home <u>quickly</u>, picking sand <u>out of</u> our hair all the way to

18   Sharla's front <u>door</u>.   <u>Though</u> we were cold and sandy, we had a <u>really</u> great

19   first day at the pool.